1000
Gaten Matarazzo Facts

Mera Wolfe

Contents

PREFACE

Think you know everything there is to know about about Gaten Matarazzo? Well, think again. 1000 Gaten Matarazzo Facts contains all you could ever wish to know about this popular young actor. Facts about Stranger Things, fashion, music, likes & dislikes, food, career, background, Broadway, Prank Encounters, lifestyle, quotes, famous friends and so much more all awaits in 1000 Gaten Matarazzo Facts. Hopefully this book will provide an entertaining and insightful extended profile of Gaten Matarazzo with plenty of fascinating trivia and things you didn't know.

1000 GATEN MATARAZZO FACTS

(1) Gaten Matarazzo was born in Connecticut in 2002. He was raised though in Little Egg Harbor Township, New Jersey.

(2) Gaten's full name is Gaetano John "Gaten" Matarazzo III.

(3) Gaten has two siblings - an older sister named Sabrina and a younger brother named Carmen.

(4) Gaten is of Italian descent.

(5) Gaten says that his sister was the person who inspired him to become a stage performer.

(6) Gaten is not related to the actress Heather Matarazzo. Heather Matarazzo (who is best known for the films Welcome to the Dollhouse, The Princess Diaries, and Scream 3) once had to deny stories she was his mother! The confusion stemmed from the fact that Gaten's real mother is also named Heather.

(7) Gaten made his stage debut on Broadway in Priscilla, Queen of the Desert in 2011.

(8) In 2014 Gaten played Gavroche/Petit Gervaisin Les Misérables at the Imperial Theatre in midtown-Manhattan.

(9) At only eleven years-old, Gaten performed six days a week and matinees for his role of Gavroche in Les Misérables while still attending school!

(10) Gaten says that Phantom of the Opera is his favourite musical.

(11) Gaten says his favourite food is his mother's mac and cheese.

(12) Gaten appeared in the NBC crime thriller The Blacklist in 2015.

(13) Gaten said his least favourite subject at school was math.

(14) Gaten can play a number of musical instruments.

(15) Gaten did his vocal training at Starlight Performing Arts Center in New Jersey.

(16) Gaten's zodiac sign is Virgo.

(17) Gaten, Caleb McLaughlin and Sadie Sink knew each other vaguely before Stranger Things from working in shows on Broadway.

(18) Gaten likes to eat oatmeal for breakfast.

(19) Gaten has a condition called cleidocranial dysplasia - a rare disorder that affects the growth of bones and teeth. "It's a condition where you're born without your collar bones — I don't have any," explained Gaten. "It affects your facial growth, your skull growth, it affects your teeth, that's why I don't have any."

(20) Gaten was cast as Dustin Henderson in Stranger Things in 2015. Dustin is a charismatic child with a quick wit and a love of science.

(21) Stranger Things is science fiction horror show created by Ross and Matt Duffer set in the 1980s. It was launched on Netflix in 2016 and is pretty much the biggest TV show in the world.

(22) Gaten originally auditioned to play Mike Wheeler in Stranger Things. He also read for the part of Lucas Sinclair.

(23) Gaten was deemed not quite right when he tested to play Mike Wheeler but the Duffer Brothers (who created Stranger Things) were so impressed by his charisma and charm they decided he simply had to be in the show.

(24) Dustin Henderson is simply a bullied overweight nerd in the pitch bible for Stranger Things. Gaten would make Dustin a much pluckier and more three dimensional character than these early sketch notes. The Duffers said that the Dustin Henderson we see in Stranger Things was completely informed by Gaten.

(25) The production of season one of Stranger things was a low-key affair with hardly any media buzz. Gaten said he had no idea if Stranger Things would find an audience or continue beyond one season but did have confidence that they were making something good.

(26) The cast in Stranger Things were not given all of the scripts for season one and had no idea how the story was going to end. They were only given a fresh script for the episode they were about to shoot.

(27) Gaten hosts the Netflix show Prank Encounters.

(28) Though he hosts his own prank show, Gaten says that Millie Bobby Brown and Noah Schnapp are the

biggest pranksters on the set of Stranger Things.

(29) Gaten has a pool table at his house and loves to shoot pool while at home.

(30) Good Housekeeping reported that babies named Dustin went up by 32% in the year after Stranger Things was released!

(31) Gaten promoted a candy called Nerd Clusters. The candy features a sweet gummy center that is covered in tangy, crunchy Nerds candy pieces. Gaten says he was happy to do this promotion because he is a candy fanatic in real life.

(32) Gaten likes watching basketball both on television and live in arenas.

(33) Gaten says that his dream role would be to play Spider-Man.

(34) Gaten said he had no idea that he wasn't competing with anyone for the part of Dustin Henderson in Stranger Things. The part was earmarked for Gaten after he read for Mike Wheeler and no one else was considered.

(35) The first scene ever shot for Stranger Things was the opening (after the prologue in the lab) of the first episode with the four boys playing Dungeon & Dragons in the Mike Wheeler basement.

(36) Gaten's voice changed so much around the time of season one of Stranger Things that he wasn't allowed to dub any of Dustin Henderson's dialogue during the ADR (Automated Dialogue Replacement) process. ADR is when actors go back to re-voice some lines that were not

picked up very well on audio.

(37) Gaten says that he likes browsing YouTube to relax and entertain himself.

(38) Given the prevalence of Broadway kids and would be singers and musicians in the cast, there is a lot of singing on the set of Stranger Things!

(39) Gaten said he has watched the Star Wars films so many times he has lost count.

(40) Gaten says he loves eating fruit - which is obviously good because it is very healthy!

(41) Gaten thinks Stranger Things is popular because it appeals to a wide demographic. "I think it's for everyone. You have adults who are nostalgic about the 80s who love it and kids who love watching other kids in shows that are not necessarily targeted at children."

(42) At the time of writing, Gaten is said to have a net worth of $4 million. It is obviously difficult to know though how much a celebrity is really worth - unless one has access to their bank statements!

(43) Gaten is a big fan of the Steven Spielberg film Saving Private Ryan.

(44) Gaten's cleidocranial dysplasia was written into his character Dustin Henderson in Stranger Things.

(45) Gaten has campaigned to raise awareness of cleidocranial dysplasia. Gaten says that many sufferers have worse cases of the condition than he does.

(46) Near the end of the Stranger Things season one finale, Mike Wheeler was supposed to carry the exhausted Eleven into the school classroom. However, Finn Wolfhard found it too difficult to carry Millie Bobby Brown so Gaten (as Dustin obviously) did it instead.

(47) The kids in Stranger Things were given relatively little makeup because the Duffers thought it would be more realistic if they had a few spots and blemishes.

(48) Gaten is a fan of the punk band Green Day. He often sports a Green Day t-shirt in photographs

(49) Gaten said that spoiler security was so tight on Stranger Things 2 he was even banned from sending his brother any texts discussing the production.

(50) Gaten is fond of peanut butter and jelly sandwiches.

(51) Gaten said he likes discovering obscure video games that aren't very famous.

(52) Gaten said that, happily, his cleidocranial dysplasia hasn't really hindered his acting career too much - though it did complicate it somewhat in the early days.

(53) Gaten says he has a sweet tooth and is a big fan of cookies.

(54) Gaten loves guacamole. Guacamole is an avocado-based dip, spread, or salad first developed in Mexico.

(55) Though set in Indiana, Stranger Things is filmed in and around Atlanta, Georgia.

(56) Dustin in Stranger Things is a fan of Three

Musketeers candy (a chocolate covered candy bar with a fluffy nougat filling). Gaten said he is also a fan of this candy.

(57) Gaten and the other children in the cast had to arrange their schooling around Stranger Things and were assigned tutors and a classroom on the set in the early seasons.

(58) Dustin has a certificate of Anti-Paranormal Proficiency in season two of Stranger Things. He is plainly a member of the Ghostbusters fan club.

(59) Gaten was in the Katy Perry music video for the song Swish Swish.

(60) Gaten carrying Millie Bobby Brown into the classroom in the finale of season one of Stranger Things was impressive because he had an injured ankle at the time.

(61) Gaten said that he shares many qualities with Dustin Henderson - including a love of science.

(62) Gaten was about seven when he first started acting and going to auditions.

(63) Gaten said that being a child actor was no picnic. Rejections are unavoidable because you are always competing with hundreds of other children for parts.

(64) Gaten attended Pinelands Regional High School in Tuckerton, New Jersey.

(65) Gaten said his favourite subject at school was history.

(66) Gaten said he isn't really interested in fame very much and just likes being an actor.

(67) Gaten once said he wanted to go to college but his acting career has obviously taken precedent and at the time f writing he has yet to do this.

(68) Gaten is a fan of Charleston Chew. Charleston Chew is a candy bar consisting of flavored nougat covered in chocolate flavor coating.

(69) Gaten has improvised a few lines as Dustin Henderson that were kept in Stranger Things because the Duffer Brothers enjoyed them.

(70) At the time of writing, Gaten's girlfriend is Lizzy Yu. Lizzy Yu is a musical theater performer and Instagram star.

(71) In season three of Stranger Things, Dustin names his radio tower 'Cerebro' after the device Professor X uses to track mutants in The X-Men.

(72) Out of the characters in Stranger Things, Dustin Henderson is the only one of the boys in the show who doesn't have any siblings.

(73) Gaten is a fan of the band Pearl Jam.

(74) The parents and siblings of the children in the cast of Stranger Things were a regular presence on the set during season one.

(75) Gaten is a big Harry Potter fan.

(76) Gaten has twice been nominated at the Teen Choice Awards for his role in Stranger Things.

(77) Gaten says The Goonies is one of his favourite movies. The Goonies is one of the many influences on Stranger Things.

(78) Gaten has had to have several surgeries as a result of his cleidocranial dysplasia.

(79) Gaten did his first Stranger things audition in New York. He was eventually flown to Los Angeles to do a final test.

(80) Gaten was the first of the kids to be cast in Stranger Things.

(81) Gaten says that Jaws is one of his favourite movies.

(82) When the pandemic shut down production on Stranger Things 4, Gaten, who suddenly found himself at a loose end, volunteered as a food runner in a Long Beach Island restaurant.

(83) In 2011, Gaten competed in a national singing competition in Connecticut and performed the vocal solo Ben. He finished in third place.

(84) A number of Dustin Henderson lookalikes were hired to promote season two of Stranger Things at Comic Con.

(85) Gaten is a fan of Eminem.

(86) The Duffers say it is a complete coincidence that many of the kids in the Stranger Things cast have a

Broadway background. Broadwy kids are obviously just good at acting.

(87) In a poll, Stranger Things came top out of Netflix shows which can be enjoyed the whole family.

(88) In 2017, Gaten became a Kid Ambassador for Holiday Inn.

(89) For his role as Dustin, Gaten was awarded with the Outstanding Performance by an Ensemble in a Drama Series at the Screen Actors Guild Awards in 2017.

(90) The many children who auditioned for Stranger Things were required to play scenes from Stand By Me and E.T. the Extra-Terrestrial.

(91) The Ghostbusters costumes the boys wear in Stranger Things 2 were really modified mechanic uniforms.

(92) Gaten, as you might expect coming from a family with some Italian heritage, is a big fan of pasta.

(93) Gaten says he has never lost his love for musical theatre and would love to return to Broadway one day.

(94) Gaten says his favourite Star Wars movie is Return of the Jedi. His second favourite is The Empire Strikes Back.

(95) Having a video game arcade in Stranger Things 2 was apparently one of the very first ideas the Duffers conceived when they began thinking about the second season although Gaten would later claim it was him who suggested having an arcade in Stranger Things 2.

(96) Gaten's favourite colour is yellow.

(97) Gaten is a big fan of Chris Pratt.

(98) Gaten says he doesn't like raw tomatoes.

(99) In 2018, Gaten and Millie Bobby Brown sent messages of support on social media to a young boy who threw a Stranger Things party that no one turned up to.

(100) Dustin wears a Science Museum of Minnesota dinosaur hoodie in Stranger Things 2. The Science Museum of Minnesota's website crashed after season two came out because the demand for these hoodies was so great.

(101) Gaten says he loves egg salad.

(102) The town of Jackson, which doubles for Hawkins, has enjoyed a nice financial boost thanks to all the visits by Stranger Things fans.

(103) At the start of Stranger Things 2, we see Dustin and the boys playing Dragon's Lair in the Palace Arcade. What we see though is not the actual game playing but merely animation that was used in advance commercials for the arcade machine.

(104) In 2015, Gaten sang the national anthem with his sister before a Mets baseball game.

(105) Gaten says he loves theatre because there is nothing quite like performing in front of a live audience.

(106) Although he started acting when he was seven,

Gaten only got his first role when he was nine. He had two tough years of auditions before he was cast in anything!

(107) Gaten said he nearly quit acting before he got his first part. The other Stranger Things kids have said this too. Many child actors have quit the business because of constant rejections. The kids in Stranger Things say that one must develop a thick skin to be a child actor because it can be a rough business.

(108) Gaten says that when he goes on holiday the most important thing to pack is a good book! His favourites are the Harry Potter series and Stephen King.

(109) Gaten said that one of his favourite places he has visited is Paris.

(110) Gaten said he has been impressed by some of the Stranger Things fan fiction he has encountered.

(111) Dustin's new invention in Stranger Things 3 deliberately looks like Randall Peltzer's electric hammer from Joe Dante's 1984 film Gremlins.

(112) As part of his auditions for Stranger Things, Gaten had to perform a scene with Finn Wolfhard (who plays Mike Wheeler in the show) to see what their chemistry was like. Their chemistry was obviously great in the audition because they were both cast in the show.

(113) Gaten was born at New London's Lawrence and Memorial Hospital.

(114) Gaten is a fan of Pokémon.

(115) Gaten enjoys drinking tea.

(116) Gaten said he was never put under any pressure to become an actor by his family and his parents told him if he ever got fed up with showbusiness or it made him unhappy he should go and do something else.

(117) Gaten said that when you are in the public eye you never really get used to being famous because it's quite a surreal and unusual situation to be in.

(118) Gaten says that no one, including the Duffers, expected Stranger Things to be such a big hit. They were aiming for it to be a cult show but to become this huge mainstream smash was beyond their wildest expectations.

(119) Gaten loves Reese's Fast Break. Reese's Fast Break is a chocolate bar. It has a milk chocolate coating over a peanut butter filling.

(120) Gaten became yet another member of the Stranger Things cast to dabble in music when he became the lead singer for a group called Work in Progress. Gaten's band is a seven-person ensemble which includes both of his siblings.

(121) Gaten said it was pretty tough and exhausting to combine acting with school but fun all the same.

(122) Gaten said that when Stranger Things came out in 2016, people at school who used to ignore him now wanted to be his friend.

(123) Gaten says that his old friends are used to him being an actor and don't treat him as if he's a celebrity.

(124) Gaten says that he doesn't really geek out when he meets famous people. The only exceptions were Mark Hamill and Harrison Ford because they were in his beloved Star Wars.

(125) Gaten says there is a lot of luck involved in being an actor. You just have to hope a lucky break goes your way and you get a part in something in the end.

(126) Gaten supplied the voice of Bubba in The Angry Birds Movie 2.

(127) Gaten is a fan of Led Zeppelin.

(128) Gaten thinks he has a lot in common with Dustin Henderson is that they both love science fiction and mysteries.

(129) Gaten says he isn't very good at cooking and doesn't cook much at all when he's at home.

(130) Gaten enjoys visiting theme parks.

(131) Gaten says he loves the eighties clothes he has to wear in Stranger Things and says costume fittings are always fun.

(132) Gaten said the one Stranger Things outfit he didn't like so much though was at the start of season three when Dustin has just come back from camp. Gaten said that Dustin's summer camp outfit was a trifle too small and tight for his tastes.

(133) Gaten wore Ted Baker Menswear at the 2017 Emmys.

(134) Gaten seems to be quite fond of bow-ties when he has to dress up for a function.

(135) Gaten loves cannolis. Cannoli are Italian pastries consisting of tube-shaped shells of fried pastry dough, filled with a sweet, creamy filling usually containing ricotta.

(136) It is Gaten who has the most lines in Stranger Things 2. His character Dustin has an impressive 356 lines in Stranger Things 2.

(137) Gaten's family run a diner called Matarazzo's Pizzeria and Restaurant in New Jersey.

(138) Gaten has been on the reality music competition show Drop the Mic.

(139) Joe Keery, who plays Steve Harrington, said he loves working with Gaten in Stranger Things. "I was so, so pumped to work with Gaten. He is just so professional. He has a profound amount of talent. For somebody his age, he has such a brilliant work ethic and is just also so humble about the whole thing. You give him two takes, and he can just nail anything you give him. And the thing I feel that works really well about Gaten, we both bring different things to the table. And maybe that's why people really enjoy watching it because it's kinda like The Odd Couple. It's this match that you didn't really even know you needed. And then when it does work out, it's just really fun to see these people from these two different worlds, who both think they have it totally figured out really help each other out."

(140) Stranger Things was going to be called Montauk

when Gaten first signed up. Montauk is a real village on the east end of the Long Island peninsula. For many years it was home to an air force base named Camp Hero. The base was originally tasked with watching out for Nazi U-boats and then became a Cold War radar station with the mission of charting the movement of any Soviet long range aircraft that might be encroaching on American airspace. The base officially closed in the early 1980s but the huge radar antenna was left standing. In 1992, a man named Preston Nichols wrote a book called The Montauk Project in which he claimed that Camp Hero was the site of secret government experiments into time travel, teleportation, ESP, monsters, space travel, and other equally unlikely areas of research.

(141) Montauk was eventually dropped as the location for the show. The Duffers, on reflection, decided a coastal shoot would present technical and logistical problems that were probably best avoided. The weather on the coast was also an obvious concern. The Duffers were as aware as anyone that shooting Jaws on Martha's Vineyard had been a nightmare for Steven Spielberg with the bad weather and tourist sailboats constantly roaming into view and ruining shots. They didn't want Montauk to be a nightmare production. The Duffers decided that the story for their show would now take place in a more generic any town USA backdrop rather than the Amity Island inspired Montauk.

(142) The cast of Stranger Things bonded very quickly on season one. The children, who aside from Gaten and Caleb McLaughlin had never met before, all became close right from the start.

(143) A new Stranger Things comic called Science Camp features Dustin away at camp.

(144) In the season one finale of Stranger Things, Dustin searches for chocolate pudding like Chunk in The Goonies.

(145) Gaten is a fan of the band Rush.

(146) Gaten's favourite character in Star Wars is Chewbacca.

(147) Gaten's sister said that his agent didn't think Gaten would get any television work because of he had a slight lisp at the time. Happily the agent was wrong about that.

(149) Gaten said it was a challenge making the transition from theatre to television. He had to adjust his style of acting because it's a completely different medium.

(150) Dustin's mother is played by a different actress in season one of Stranger Things. Tabitha Kilgore appears briefly as Mrs Henderson during Will's funeral. Catherine Curtin would take over the role in season two.

(151) Gaten says that despite all the monsters and horror elements in Stranger Things he has never been scared during filming.

(152) Dustin brings some trail mix for the Operation Mirkwood quest in season one of Stranger Things. Trail mix is typically a combination of granola, dried fruit, and nuts.

(153) Dustin has been to Camp Know Where at the start of season three of Stranger Things. Camp Nowhere is a 1994 film starring Christopher Lloyd.

(154) When Dustin can't find anyone to dance with in the Stranger Things 2 finale, he is saved by Nancy - who not only dances with him but provides some words of wisdom. Ross Duffer said this scene was based on a female cousin of his doing the same thing when he was a child.

(155) In season two of Stranger Things, Dustin (much to the dismay of Steve) adopts a growl when he displays his 'pearls' (teeth). This was partly inspired by Gaten Matarazzo's mimicry of Chewbacca from Star Wars.

(156) Gaten said he has learned a lot about acting by working with David Harbour and Winona Ryder in Stranger Things.

(157) Stranger Things 2 began production with a secret codename in an attempt to avoid media attention and potential spoilers.

(158) Gaten has appeared in Cinderella on the stage.

(159) Gaten's credits include Lip Sync Battle.

(160) Gaten has done some voice acting for a film called Hump. Simon Pegg is also a vice actor in this movie.

(161) Dustin is wearing a Castroville Artichoke Festival t-shirt in the last two episodes of season one of Stranger Things.

(162) Gaten visited the Wizarding World of Harry Potter at Universal Orlando in 2021 and sampled some butterbeer. Butterbeer at this theme park is cream soda-meets-butterscotch flavor with a sweet whipped topping.

(163) Gaten is a fan of the band My Chemical Romance.

(164) Gaten's music group has done some Pearl Jam covers.

(165) Gaten said the film Insidious is one of his favourite scary movies.

(166) Gaten said he loves snickerdoodles. A snickerdoodle is a type of cookie made with butter or oil, sugar, salt, and flour, and rolled in cinnamon sugar.

(167) Priah Ferguson, who plays Eric, says that Gaten is the biggest real life nerd in the Stranger Things cast. "[I hope he doesn't] get mad or offended, but it would probably be Gaten. His personality matches up with his character - he has a little bit of quirkiness to him, which is fine. I have a little bit of quirkiness to myself!"

(168) Gaten says he doesn't like jello.

(169) Dustin calls himself 'Gold Leader' on the walkie-talkie when he returns from camp in Stranger Things 3 and is trying to contact his friends. Gold Leader is the callsign of Lando Calrissian in Return of the Jedi.

(170) Dungeons & Dragons is a roll the dice fantasy board game first released in 1974. The Duffers never played this game as children but wanted to use it as a means to convey the friendship of the boys in Stranger Things. The children in Stranger Things use Dungeons & Dragons terms to understand the strange happenings in Hawkins and this transfers as a type of shorthand to convey information to the viewer too. The game the boys are playing at the start of The Vanishing of Will Byers also foreshadows the plot of season one.

(171) When his toys come to life (thanks to Eleven) in the first episode of the 1985 set Stranger Things 3, we see that Dustin has a Transformer Ultra Magnus. This toy was not released in the United States until 1986. We can only presume Dustin had a Japanese version imported!

(172) A record 26.4 million users watched Stranger Things 3 the weekend of its release, and 824,000 binged all eight episodes on the day of its debut.

(173) Gaten says the Dustin/Erica dynamic in Stranger Things 3 is a bit like Steve's friendship with Dustin. "They learn that they actually have a lot in common, kind of like Dustin and Steve. Instead of Dustin being the Padawan, now Erica's the Padawan and Dustin's the master."

(174) Todd Yellin, Netflix's VP of product innovation, claims that Stranger Things is so popular they even had a viewer in Antarctica!

(175) It was Gaten's idea for his character Dustin Henderson to have cleidocranial dysplasia. He felt it would help raise awareness for the condition.

(176) Millie Bobby Brown said the boys in Stranger Things mostly talk about video games off camera when they are shooting.

(177) Gaten said it's difficult sometimes to dress up for red carpets because he's more at home in a t-shirt.

(178) In the Stranger Things season two episode The Pollywog, Dustin consults a field guide to reptiles and amphibians and suggests Indirana semipalmata as the species of frog that Dart could be. However, Indirana

semipalmata wasn't classified as a term until 1986.

(179) Gaten is a producer on his show Prank Encounters.

(180) Joe Keery's Steve Harrington began the second season of Stranger Things in a couple with Nancy but the Duffers separated them because they wanted to put Jonathan and Nancy together. They wanted to use Jonathan and Nancy to get justice for Barb's death and also express their romantic feelings for one another. This left the character of Steve Harrington and Joe Keery with very little to do for the rest of the season. On a whim, the Duffers put Steve with Dustin for a few scenes and were so delighted with the comic chemistry between Joe Keery and Gaten they leant on this dynamic for the rest of the season.

(181) Gaten is about 5'5 tall.

(182) The Stranger Things kids watched the Superbowl teaser for Stranger Things 2 together at a special party.

(183) Gaten is famously polite and patient when it comes to signing autographs and talking to fans.

(184) Gaten said he loves chocolate cake.

(185) Gaten is a fan of the band Foo Fighters.

(186) Gaten said he used to find the Count from Sesame Street quite scary when he was a kid.

(187) The Duffers say the kids swear much more in real life than they do in Stranger Things!

(188) Millie Bobby Brown said that when the boys got on

her nerves shooting the first season of Stranger Things she would seek sanctuary in Winona Ryder's trailer.

(189) The Duffers say that their direction notes in season one included reminders to the kids not to slap each other before takes!

(190) There has been Stranger Things Minecraft and Stranger Things Lego.

(191) Joe Keery says he learned a lot about acting from the kids in Stranger Things.

(192) An early idea the Duffers had for Stranger Things 2 was Dustin Henderson adopting or encountering some sort of strange creature from the Upside Down and discovering (like Zach Galligan in Gremlins or the crew of the Nostromo) that this creature is far more trouble and much more dangerous then he ever expected. They liked this idea because it would give Dustin his own plot arc in Stranger Things 2. The Duffers loved Gaten's performance in season one and wanted Dustin Henderson to have plenty of dialogue and screen time in season two.

(193) Benny Hammond, the diner owner who is killed by Connie Frazier in the first episode of Stranger Things, was named Benny Henderson in the pilot script. This would appear to suggest that Benny might originally have been conceived as a relative of Dustin.

(194) When Dustin locates the missing Dart in the school in season two of Stranger Things, you might notice the word EVIL scrawled on the wall. This is a less than subtle visual clue that Dustin has made a big mistake adopting Dart.

(195) Gaten says he really loves the night shoots on Stranger Things. "I actually like doing the night shoots more, I feel more energized during them. All the kids love doing them."

(196) Dustin speculates the Soviets might be dabbling in Promethium in Stranger Things 3. Promethium is the substance used to build the superhero Cyborg in DC Comics.

(197) Dustin's sneakers in season one of Stranger Things are K-Swiss Heaven S.

(198) Gaten is a fan of penne with a vodka sauce. Penne alla vodka is tender penne pasta tossed in a rich and delicious tomato, vodka and cream sauce.

(199) Dustin has a Waupaca, Wis t-shirt in the first season Stranger Things episode The Flea and the Acrobat. This is the name of an iron foundry.

(200) The boys had a fit of the giggles shooting the Dungeons & Dragons scene that begins Stranger Things.

(201) Gaten says he would open to the idea of a Steve/Dustin spin-off show when Stranger Things ends.

(202) There was a slight battle between Netflix and the Duffers on Stranger Things 2 when it came to swearing. Netflix wanted to do alternative takes of the scenes where the kids swear so that bad language was very minimal. The kids in the cast hated this idea because they thought scenes were much funnier with a few stray cuss words by their characters. The Duffers also preferred the takes with the odd cuss word so in the end Netflix conceded.

(203) Gaten said he would be completely up for playing
Obi-Wan Kenobi in a Star Wars film when he's mature
enough for the part.

(204) Universal Studios' Halloween Horror Nights
devoted a spooky maze to Stranger Things in 2019.

(205) Mike's line ("Holy s***! What happened to you?")
to Dustin at the Snow Ball dance in Stranger Things 2 is
the same as a line Finn Wolfhard has as Richie to Ben
Hanscom in the film IT.

(206) Gaten says that the music video for Michael
Jackson's Thriller song scared him when he was younger.
Thriller is a legendary horror themed music video
directed by John Landis. It features zombies and
werewolves.

(207) Gaten's hair is naturally curly.

(208) Gaten said that he never thought he'd end up
working in television. He thought he would just be a stage
actor.

(209) Stranger Things producer and director Shawn Levy
said of Gaten - "The second Gaten walked in, we were
like, Okay well we're done looking for Dustin, because
he's in the room with us right frickin' now. I remember
that being the most un-debatable casting decision. He has
the greatest face on planet Earth, and he has such a
natural comedic instinct that we needed in that group. We
knew Mike was going to be something of a leader. We
knew Lucas was dealing with suspicion and anger. So we
needed a force of pure positivity and levity, and Gaten
walked in with that."

(210) When he auditioned to be in Stranger Things, Gaten read lines that were written for the character of Lucas Sinclair.

(211) Gaten loves the game Mario Kart.

(212) Gaten said that when he took a job as a food runner at a diner while there was a hiatus on the production of Stranger Things 4, he tried to be incognito by wearing a hat but it didn't work. The customers knew who he was straight away!

(213) Gaten is till very active and visible in his local community. He hasn't moved to Hollywood yet.

(214) Gaten is a genuine small town kid. His home town only has a population of about 20,000.

(215) Gaten has attended many conventions since Stranger Things became a hit show.

(216) Gaten is a big fan of pretzels.

(217) Gaten says he is always very careful about what he says and how he behaves because of his status as a public figure.

(218) Gaten is a fan of Dungeons & Dragons in real life too.

(219) Gaten's younger brother is also an actor.

(220) Gaten is a fan of The Black Keys.

(221) Gaten appeared in Computer Games' Lost Boys Life

video.

(222) Gaten has 313 lines in Stranger Things 3. This ranks him third in the actors with the most lines in the third season.

(223) When he appeared in The Blacklist in 2015, Gaten played a character called Finn. This was quite spooky given that Finn Wolfhard would be one of his main co-stars in Stranger Things a year later.

(224) Gaten says that cleidocranial dysplasia is very rare and that he has a non-genetic version.

(225) Gaten likes quinoa burgers.

(226) Look fast and you will see Dustin's hat from previous seasons in Suzie's bedroom in the Stranger Things 3 finale.

(227) Gaten performed a golf cart duet with Kelly Clarkson for WE Day Toronto 2017.

(228) At the time of writing, Gaten has 13.8 million Instagram followers.

(229) Most of the networks who rejected Stranger Things wanted the show to lose the kids and focus on Hopper as the central character. These networks obviously made a huge mistake by rejecting the show. They must have been kicking themselves when Stranger Things became an incredible hit for Netflix.

(230) Gaten is a fan of Bon Jovi.

(231) Gaten said if he could have any one special ability it

would be shapeshifting so he could turn into different types of animals!

(232) According to the Hollywood Reporter, the child actors in Stranger Things were paid $20,000 an episode in season one.

(233) It was widely reported that the cast received hefty pay rises for Stranger Things 3 and that the kids (or teenagers as they were now) were on $250,000 an episode (a massive increase from the $20,000 an episode the kids were supposedly on in season one).

(234) Gaten is a big fan of the game Pac-Man.

(235) Gaten was twelve years-old when he was cast as Dustin Henderson in Stranger Things.

(236) Gaten went through three auditions before he was cast as Dustin Henderson in Stranger Things.

(237) Gaten said that when he was cast in Stranger things he had to keep it a secret and was only allowed to tell his immediate family.

(238) Gaten said of Dustin Henderson in season one of Stranger Things - "I would describe Dustin's role in the pack as the glue that kind of holds everybody together. He is the voice of reason and, very often, the peacemaker."

(239) Gaten has designed a t-shirt in support of the Cleidocranial Dysplasia charity CCD Smiles.

(240) Gaten is a big fan of baseball.

(241) Gaten celebrated his 14th birthday with a special

donut cake!

(242) Gaten is a fan of milkshakes.

(243) Gaten is a big fan of board games.

(244) In 2019, Gaten attended junior Prom with his girlfriend Lizzy Yu.

(245) Gaten likes to visit Tuckerton Seaport Haunted Seaport at Halloween. This is a spooky local attraction where he lives.

(246) Gaten says it is quite surreal to be recognised by people in public - even when he is abroad.

(247) Gaten has appeared on a number of talk shows - including Jimmy Fallon and Kelly Ripa.

(248) Gaten's family moved to New Jersey to be closer to his mother's parents.

(249) Gaten doesn't act like a famous person at all. It is still possible to bump into him in a store or something ordinary like that.

(250) In the bike chase in season one of Stranger Things, the boys mention "Elm and Cherry" as a meeting point. This seems a likely reference to A Nightmare On Elm Street.

(251) Gaten loves the Rise of the Resistance ride at Walt Disney World.

(252) Gaten loves cats.

(253) Gaten says he prefers acting to singing.

(254) Gaten said he has been impressed by the way the Duffers write in the fact that the younger cast members grew up fast over the course of the show. "As we are growing older as people, we have to grow older as characters," he continued. "[Creators Matt and Ross Duffer are] confronted by this issue, but they embrace it and they use it to their advantage. And they don't freak out when we get taller or when our voices drop or anything like that. They use it as ammunition for their writing."

(255) Gaten says he is probably the biggest nerd in the Stranger Things cast although he thinks that Finn Wolfhard runs him pretty close.

(256) Gaten says that being in Stranger Things is the coolest job on earth.

(257) The finale of Stranger Things 3 features an unexpected duet when Suzie makes Dustin sing the theme song to The Neverending Story with her before she will divulge the Planck's constant numbers for the Russian code. The song was composed by Giorgio Moroder and originally sung by sung by Limahl with Beth Anderson. Gaten had never heard of The Neverending Story and was apprehensive about having to sing. Gabriella Pizzolo, by contrast, was already a fan of the song and perfectly happy to sing it on the show. Gaten and Pizzolo both wore an earpiece during the song so they could hear one another and match their harmonies.

(258) Gaten is a fan of Billie Joe Armstrong.

(259) Because of his cleidocranial dysplasia, Gaten wears

dentures in Stranger Things.

(260) Gaten is interested in digital photography.

(261) Gaten said that when he first went up for the part of
Dustin in Stranger Things the character wasn't even even
going to be a cast regular. This obviously all changed
though.

(262) There is a scientific goof regarding the Planck
constant (a physical constant that is the quantum of
electromagnetic action) in Stranger Things 3. Suzie gives
Dustin the 2017 value of Planck's constant when, as this
was 1985, she should have given him the 1973 value.

(263) The Duffers play spooky music on the set of
Starnger Things to get the actors in the right mood to
convey fear and tension for scary scenes.

(264) When Gaten and some of the cast and crew visited
the White House after the first season of Stranger Things
they learned that President Obama was a big fan of the
show.

(265) The real shooting location for Hawkins High School
in Stranger Things is the Patrick Henry High School in
Atlanta, Georgia.

(266) Gaten has appeared in videos promoting safe teen
driving in his native New Jersey.

(267) Gaten is a big fan of the vintage arcade game
Galaga.

(268) Gaten said he first watched the original Star Wars
film when he was four years-old.

(269) Gaten appeared in the music video for Green Day's
Meet Me on the Roof.

(270) Gaten is a fan of the 70s and 80s rock band Queen.

(271) Gaten says he leaves his red carpet outfits to his
fashion stylist.

(272) The TRC-214 walkie-talkies in Stranger Things
might be a slight mistake as they only started being listed
in Radio Shack's 1985 catalogue - two years after season
one takes place.

(273) Video arcade games in the 1980s used cathode ray
tube (CRT) monitors - not flat-panel LCD screens as seen
in the arcade scenes in Stranger Things 2.

(274) The junkyard scene in The Bathtub episode of
Stranger Things where the kids hide in the rusted bus was
tough to shoot because the boys kept breaking wind!

(275) Gaten got his high school diploma.

(276) Gaten says he loves most types of pudding -
especially chocolate ones.

(277) Gaten attended a dance school in Tuckerton.

(278) Dustin tells his friends early on in Stranger Things
3 that his girlfriend Suzie is 'hotter' than Phoebe Cates.
Phoebe Cates is best known for her role in Joe Dante's
Gremlins.

(279) Gaten uses AXE Natural Look Understated Cream
on his hair.

(280) Gaten is a fan of the pop band Paramore.

(281) Gaten has to endure a lot of early mornings during the production of Stranger Things. Often he has to be on the set at 6am to start work.

(282) Gaten thinks he had to grow up faster than most kids because he's been working with adults for a long time.

(283) Gaten said he once got the autograph of Star Wars creator George Lucas in Los Angeles. He said George Lucas didn't know who he was he was at first but then clocked that Gaten was from Stranger Things.

(284) Gaten has supported a nonprofit restaurant called Soul Kitchen whose donated proceeds go toward helping individuals struggling with food insecurity.

(285) Gaten is a fan of Eddie Vedder.

(286) Stranger Things 3 has the characters drinking New Coke. In 1985 Coca-Cola was rebranded as New Coke and the formula tweaked to make it sweeter and more syrupy like Pepsi. There were howls of protests from people who liked Coca-Cola exactly as it was and didn't understand why it had to change. The old formula was eventually brought back and the company lost tens of millions of dollars in unsold bottles of New Coke.

(287) Dustin calls one of the teams in Stranger Things 3 the 'Griswold family'. The Griswolds are a fictional family that featured in the 1983 comedy film National Lampoon's Vacation. Chevy Chase played the head of the family, the hapless Clark Griswold. The sequel, National

Lampoon's European Vacation, arrived in 1985. The Griswolds returned in 1989's National Lampoon's Christmas Vacation, and then in 1997's Vegas Vacation.

(288) The scene in Stranger Things 3 where Dustin's toys come to life is very similar to a scene in the 1985 fantasy film Making Contact by Roland Emmerich.

(289) Gaten is a big fan of pizza.

(290) Steve and Dustin are bemused by a Jazzercise class in Stranger Things 3. Jazzercise is a fusion of dance and fitness created in 1969.

(291) Gaten loves chocolate brownies.

(292) In a 2019 poll by MoffettNathanson of Netflix's U.S. subscribers, Stranger Things was - surprisingly - not the most popular Netflix show. It was voted second most popular behind Orange Is the New Black.

(293) The kids in Stranger Things went out trick or treating together at Halloween for real the year that Stranger Things 2 came out. Surprisingly though, they said they were not recognised by anyone!

(294) Joe Keery says that the kids in the Stranger Things cast kicked him out of their group chat for being too old!

(295) The source of Dustin's 'totally tubular' refrain in Stranger Things 2 is probably Frank Zappa's 1982 Valley Girl single.

(296) Ham radio, as featured most notably in season one of Stranger Things, can provide an important means of communication in a time of crisis. After Hurricane

Andrew struck South Florida in 1992, the utility grid was destroyed over hundreds of square miles. All cellular towers and antennas were blown down. Only amateur radio, the Citizens Radio Service ("Citizens Band"), and a few isolated pay phones with underground lines provided communication between the outside world and the public in the affected area.

(297) You can now buy a Retro VHS Dustin Henderson Inspired Lamp!

(298) Gaten says his ideal movie would be Star Wars combined with Harry Potter.

(299) Dustin complains about Nilla Wafers not being real ones at the funeral of Will Byers in season one of Stranger Things. Nilla Wafers are wafer style cookies. They are often used in banana pudding recipes.

(300) Dustin claims he can manipulate his body like Gumby in Stranger Things 3. Gumby is a famous clay animation character.

(301) Stranger Things has won four Fangoria Chainsaw Awards.

(302) The Weirdo On Maple Street episode of Stranger Things finds Dustin worrying that Eleven might be an escaped lunatic like Michael Myers. Michael Myers is the murderous antagonist of the Halloween horror film franchise.

(303) It took a month to design the models for how the Demogorgon would look in Stranger Things.

(304) Gaten says he is a dog person and loves dogs.

(305) Gaten and the kids from Stranger Things handed out peanut butter and jelly sandwiches to the audience at the 68th Annual Primetime Emmy Awards.

(306) In 2019, Sadie Sink, Gaten, and Finn Wolfhard attended a performance of The Book Of Mormon in New York.

(307) Gaten says Secret Santa is a tradition with the kids in his family.

(308) Gaten says the handshake between Dustin and Steve when they are reunited at the start of Stranger Things 3 was something him and Joe Keery came up with.

(309) The Duffers and Shawn Levy had to ask permission from Dan Aykroyd and Ivan Reitman (Aykroyd and Reitman held the rights to Ghostbusters) to put Gaten and the boys in Stranger Things 2 in Ghostbusters costumes. Aykroyd was a fan of Stranger Things so this didn't turn out to be a problem and permission was granted.

(310) Dustin Henderson unwittingly adopting a potentially dangerous creature from the Upside Down was pretty much one of the first ideas the Duffers had when they started writing Stranger Things 2.

(311) Gaten says that a lot of his own food obsessions were written into the character of Dustin Henderson.

(312) Mr Clarke actor Randy Havens said that on season one of Stranger Things it was hard not to fluff takes because the kids always made him laugh.

(313) Gaten has blue eyes.

(314) Gaten doesn't come from a showbusiness family.
His mother liked acting and singing when she was
younger but she wasn't a professional actor.

(315) The production team on Stranger Things had to find
a number of vintage period accurate board games to put
in the Wheeler basement and bedrooms of the boys.

(316) Gaten has appeared in the TV show Ridiculousness.
Ridiculousness is an American comedy clip show.

(317) Though it proved divisive to fans and audiences,
Gaten said he was a big fan of the film The Last Jedi.

(318) Gaten is a fan of chocolate milk. He likes to dunk
cookies in it.

(319) Gaten is a fan of Dog with a Blog. Dog with a Blog is
a comedy television series that aired on Disney Channel
from 2012 to 2015.

(320) Gaten's natural hair colour is brown.

(321) Gatens says that Switzerland is one of his favourite
countries out of those he has visited.

(322) There have been a number of Stranger Things pop
up bars around the world.

(323) Stranger Things merchandise now includes a
Demogorgon hat designed for dogs.

(324) David Harbour (who plays Chief Hopper) said
Gaten and the kids were bemused by the 1980s

telephones when they saw the Stranger Things sets for the first time.

(325) Gaten says that he has a love/hate relationship with social media. He thinks it can be a positive thing for connections and work and highlighting good causes but unfortunately there is also a lot of negativity and meanness in these places.

(326) In the school scenes in Stranger things 2 where Dustin's pet Dart is loose, the kids had to act with a rubber model. Dart was conveyed through special effects in post-production.

(327) Dustin and Will reference the comic X-Men-134 in episode one of Stranger Things. This is the Dark Phoenix storyline - one of the inspirations for Eleven.

(328) Gaten has done a commercial for Old Navy. This is a clothing company owned by Gap.

(329) Gaten says he is open to a musical collaboration with Stranger Things co-star Finn Wolfhard. Finn has been in two bands himself.

(330) Gaten's band Work in Progress performed two sold out shows at the end of 2017 at The Stone Pony in Asbury Park, NJ.

(331) Gaten enjoys visiting the Wildwood Boardwalk in Jersey. The Wildwood Boardwalk features several amusement parks, water parks, an aquarium, and shops, most notably three piers collectively known as Morey's Piers.

(332) Gaten loves going on roller coasters at theme parks.

He has often done this with the other Stranger Things kids.

(333) Dustin's puffed up hair at the Snow Ball in Stranger Things 2 is based on Jon Cryer in the John Hughes film Pretty in Pink.

(334) Gaten says his favourite Stranger Things fan theory is that Dustin's girlfriend Suzie is a Soviet spy!

(335) Gaten is a fan of the film The Lighthouse.

(336) Gaten says he prefers Marvel to DC.

(337) Gaten says that New York is his favourite city.

(338) Gaten enjoys rock climbing when he has the time.

(339) Gaten is a fan of the horror movie Hereditary.

(340) Gaten said one his favourite scenes in Stranger Things was in season one when Eleven uses her powers to make the lab van flip up in the air during the cycle chase.

(341) Gaten is a fan of the Nightmare On Elm Street movies.

(342) The 3 Musketeers candy bar is known as a Milky Way in some other parts of the world.

(343) At the start of Stranger Things 2, Dustin fails to get the princess when he plays Dragon's Lair. This foreshadows the fact that he won't win the heart of Max.

(344) Gaten's band perform a lot of covers. The artists they have covered included Nick Drake and Arctic

Monkeys.

(345) Gaten said he enjoyed visiting Italy and even met some relatives there.

(346) Gaten is a fan of the Friday the 13th horror movies.

(347) Dustin coins a hill Weathertop in season three of Stranger Things. This a name from The Lord of the Rings.

(348) Joe Keery said he loves the fact that Stranger Things throws up some pairings you wouldn't necessarily expect - like Steve & Dustin.

(349) The boys in Stranger Things use Telex Headsets on the ham radio.

(350) The walkie-talkies the boys have in Stranger Things usually had a radius of one mile.

(351) In the original plan for the Stranger Things season three finale, Dustin and Suzie were going to sing the Ent song from Lord Of The Rings rather than The NeverEnding Story. Matt Duffer said they abandoned this idea when they heard that Amazon were making a Lord of the Rings television series.

(352) The kids in the Stranger Things cast think that the mall they used to film season three might be haunted. This is probably because a dead body was found there once when it was derelict.

(353) The scene in Stranger Things 3 where the kids push Dustin's radio tower aloft in Suzie, Do You Copy? appears to be based on the World War 2 photograph of the American flag being raised atop Mount Suribachi at the

Battle of Iwo Jima.

(354) In October, 2021, Gaten posed for a photo with two local cops who recognised him in a store!

(355) Gaten got into acting by accident really because he was tagging along with his sister when an agent asked him if he'd like to do some acting. Gaten thought it sounded like fun and so decided to give it a whirl. That was obviously an excellent decision because it made him a millionaire in the end!

(356) Before he became famous in Stranger Things, Gaten appeared in the Radio City Christmas Spectacular. The Christmas Spectacular Starring the Radio City Rockettes is an annual musical holiday stage show presented at Radio City Music Hall in New York City.

(357) The kids (now teenagers) in Stranger Things have their trailers close to one another on the set.

(358) When Gaten was appearing on Broadway he had to do his school homework backstage in the theatre.

(359) Gaten said that Dustin Henderson only had two lines in the first script he read for Stranger Things (or Montauk as it would have been called at the time). The character of Dustin was obviously expanded into a much bigger part.

(360) The boys' trick or treat haul in season two of Stranger Things appears to include a Mr. Goodbar. Mr. Goodbar is a candy bar containing peanuts and chocolate. It's easy to spot because of the yellow wrapper.

(361) Gaten, as we have noted, says he isn't a great cook

but thinks he does make a good mac and cheese.

(362) Gaten says his agent was quite annoyed when he was cast as Dustin rather than Mike or Lucas in Stranger Things because the agent presumed the part of Dustin was quite a minor part. It all turned out fine in the end.

(363) The name the boys give their mission to find Will Byers in season one of Stranger Things is Operation Mirkwood. Mirkwood was a great forest in Middle-earth in the books of Tolkien. Dustin bringing all the food for Operation Mirkwood is a flip of the boys in Stand By Me forgetting to bring any food when they set off on their quest to find the body in the woods.

(364) Gaten says the cast members in Stranger Things often Facetime one another sometimes because they all live so far away. Gaten is in New Jersey, Finn in Canada, and Millie often in England.

(365) Gaten said that as a kid it was never his ambition to become an actor. It was just something he fell into by accident.

(366) When it comes to Harry Potter, Gaten thinks he is a Hufflepuff.

(367) Gaten is a big fan of The Lego Movie.

(368) There was some criticism of Gaten's Netflix show Prank Encounters because the prank 'victims' were unemployed people who thought they were taking up a job. Gaten defended the show by saying that all the participants knew they were only being hired for one day.

(369) Gaten said he enjoyed visiting a traditional English

pub when he was in London to promote Stranger Things.

(370) Gaten said his Screen Actors Guild Award ended up at his grandparents house.

(371) The creators of the show had originally pitched Stranger Things as an anthology but had this idea shot down by Netflix. Netflix didn't think it was a great idea. As for future seasons done as self-contained anthologies (in the vein of shows like American Horror Story or Fargo), all agreed in the end that it would have been insane to invest so much in this cast (and especially these kids) and then have a completely fresh slate of characters in the next season. An anthology approach would beg too many questions. Move the action to another town? A time jump to another era? Is the big threat the Upside Down again or some fresh supernatural conundrum? Stranger Things would have been in a terrible quagmire suddenly having to conjure a new cast as loveable and talented as the one they already had. It would have been madness to discard them and shoot season two as an anthology with all new characters. The heart of the show would be gone. It would be positively certifiable not to use fantastic actors like David Harbour and Millie Bobby Brown again. Imagine a new season of Stranger Things with no Gaten Matarazzo. Unthinkable!

(372) One advantage season two of Stranger Things had was that the children in the cast didn't seem to have changed too much at all since season one. They still looked like little kids. This was no longer the case by the time Stranger Things 3 later went into production.

(373) Gaten had to do a lot of his school work privately with a tutor because of his commitments on Stranger Things.

(374) When the boys discuss their Dungeons & Dragons campaign at the end of season one of Stranger Things and lament the fact that it wasn't longer, the subtext is clearly the fact that Stranger Things only had eight episodes.

(375) David Harbour said it was no picnic working with a bunch of kids on season one of Stranger Things. "I was joking before but it's the farting that goes on with twelve-year-olds. The amount of bodily functions they can't control is amazing. It's all kinds of boogers. When you go to work you should not have to deal with someone like — yeah, it was bad. There are little moments of weirdness. It's great and it's horrible because you want to sort of get your workday done and they're sort of crazy children."

(376) Gaten said that when they were shooting season one of Stranger Things there were a few mishaps with the long antenna on the walkie-talkies. He said Millie Bobby Brown got hit a few times!

(377) One of the episodes in Stranger Things 2 is called The Pollywog. A pollywog is a larval frog or toad, polliwog, tadpole, amphibia, class Amphibia - the class of vertebrates that live on land but breed in water.

(378) Gaten said that acting stopped becoming a hobby for him when he signed his first contract.

(379) The source of Dustin's 'totally tubular' refrain in Stranger Things 2 is probably Frank Zappa's 1982 Valley Girl single.

(380) The season one finale of Stranger Things apparently created a surge in demand for chocolate pudding.

(381) Gaten said that Charlie Heaton is the biggest corpser on the Stranger Things set in that he gets the giggles during a take.

(382) In the first season of Stranger Things, Dustin telephones Mr Clarke to ask him how one would go about constructing a sensory deprivation chamber. Mr Clarke is at home watching John Carpenter's The Thing on video. This fun cultural reference could be construed as a minor mistake though because season one is set in 1983 and John Carpenter's The Thing was not available on home video until 1984.

(383) Hasbro released a retro handheld Stranger Things game where you could play the likes of Dig Dug and Pac-Man.

(384) In 2017, a Stranger Things computer game was made by by Texas studio BonusXP, Inc. and published by Netflix. The game was deliberately retro.

(385) Gaten said he enjoyed visiting Finland although he did find it a bit chilly.

(386) Gaten is a fan of the horror movie Midsommar.

(387) Gaten said the cat who played Mews in Stranger Things 2 is his favourite co-star.

(388) Gaten said that if he wasn't an actor he would have liked to work with animals.

(389) Gaten says that gingerbread baking in the oven is his favourite smell.

(390) Gaten's fame has been a boost for the family pizza business because Stranger Things fans go there in the hope of seeing him.

(391) Gaten thinks that you only really need your family to have a nice vacation. "You don't need expensive things or going on super big adventures, you just need to make sure that you have time to spend with your family without worrying about work or school or anything and just be with them."

(392) You may notice that Dustin's bike is made up of two different colours in Stranger Things. "With Dustin's bike, we decided he was sort of a klutz. So we painted his bike but never finished it, and that's why his bike is two colours," said propmaster Lynda Reiss.

(393) When the boys and Eleven walk the train tracks in the woods during season one of Stranger Things this is an obvious reference to the film Stand By Me.

(394) A number of gamers think the Duffers might have been influenced by a Super Nintendo video game called Earthbound. Earthbound is a 1994 game about a girl with psychokinetic powers and kids on bikes having to save the universe.

(395) Gaten has done a FiOS commercial. This is an internet supplier.

(396) The PEZ dispenser Dustin brings along with the food in his backpack to search for Will in season one of Stranger Things is a Jack in the Box clown. This is a mistake as it was made in 1999.

(397) It is often reported that Netflix vaguely floated the

idea of shooting Stranger Things 2 and Stranger Things 3 back to back in the same fashion that Back to the Future Part II and Back to the Future Part III were shot back to back in the late 1980s. This approach would have mitigated some of the costs (in that you would get more value for money out of any expensive sets that had to constructed) of producing the show. Netflix obviously wanted some new Stranger Things episodes for their streaming service and the prospect of having two brand new seasons of Stranger Things up their sleeve must have sounded like Christmas to the executives. One other speculative factor in this suggestion was the desire to get more Stranger Things in the can before those cute kids that everyone loved in season one grew up too much. The Duffers and Shawn Levy were never tempted by any suggestion of shooting seasons of Stranger Things back to back. They thought the high standards set by season one might suffer if they had to write and produce sixteen episodes instead of eight. Besides, they didn't really care if the kids started growing up. They would simply write this into the show.

(398) A clothing store in Oxford Street in London had a Stranger Things themed makeover to mark the release of season two.

(399) Gaten said he doesn't like putting too much product in his hair because he wants it to look as natural as possible.

(400) The Duffers say there were no alternatives to the child actors they cast in Stranger Things. They felt they had found the only children capable of playing these parts.

(401) Gaten said he doesn't think he'll always be an actor.

He said he would like to work behind the camera one day.

(402) Although it is an anachronism for the arcade machines in Stranger Things 2 to have LCD screens (as opposed to cathode ray tube monitors) it was probably unavoidable because cathode ray tube monitors are difficult to capture perfectly when shot on film.

(403) Gaten is a fan of Fall Out Boy.

(404) Gaten wore sneakers at the 2018 Emmys. The sneakers promoted the charity CCD Smiles.

(405) Gaten teamed up with Ninja for a Stranger Things themed Dead By Daylight at Halloween 2020.

(406) Fancasting sites think Gaten would make a good Pugsley Addams in The Addmas Family.

(407) During a 2017 Motown parody with James Corden, Gaten sang with Stranger Things costars Finn Wolfhard, Caleb McLaughlin, and Noah Schnapp,

(408) Gaten is a fan of the comic actor Sacha Baron Cohen.

(409) Dustin is the character with the third most amount of lines in season one of Stranger Things. Surprisingly, he has more dialogue than Joyce and Hopper - who are in fourth and fifth place respectively.

(410) Gaten is a fan of popcorn.

(411) A cap signed by Gaten can sell for about $150 online.

(412) There is of course a Dustin Henderson Funko Pop.

(413) Gaten said that working in his family business has taught him how to make a very good pizza.

(414) Dustin and the boys use the term 'Code Red' on their walkie-talkies in Stranger Things to signify an emergency situation.

(415) The Palace Arcade in Stranger Things 2 is named after the 20 Grand Palace Arcade in the 1983 Cold War teen fantasy film WarGames.

(416) The games in the arcade built for Stranger Things 2 were all playable. The cast and crew were allowed to play on the games between takes. The arcade was a renovated laundromat located on 6500 Church Street in Douglasville, Georgia. The local people in Douglasville were said to be disappointed when they learned the arcade was not permanent and only for scenes in Stranger Things 2. It was so authentic they thought it was a real arcade someone had opened.

(417) There is a Buzz Lightyear doll in Dustin's room in Stranger Things 2. Toy Story was still over ten years away from release though in 1984.

(418) The Stranger Things special effects team found it complicated to make Dustin's pet Demogorgon Dart seem endearing because Demogorgons have no eyes.

(419) Stranger Things is scary but not TOO scary. The intention was to be like a PG-13 horror/fantasy film.

(420) Dustin wears his Ghostbusters sneakers to the Snowball dance in Stranger Things 2.

(421) Gaten is supposedly a vegetarian. He has eaten burgers on YouTube though. Maybe he became a vegetarian later?

(422) The broadcast Dustin intercepts in Stranger Things 3 plays Daisy Bell from 2001: A Space Odyssey.

(423) Gaten's sister started a Facebook campaign to raise money for cleidocranial dysostosis.

(424) Gaten is a fan of the TV show 13 Reasons Why.

(425) Gaten has performed at the Hollywood Bowl in Los Angeles.

(426) Gaten wears spectacles in real life.

(427) Gaten said it was very surreal to go to the White House and meet President Obama.

(428) Gaten's name is pronounced GAY-ten Mat-ah-RAH-zo.

(429) Gaten can sometimes be seen attending ice hockey games in New York.

(430) One of Gaten's dogs is named Mattie.

(431) Gaten thinks that he shares a sarcastic sense of humour with his Stranger Things character Dustin Henderson.

(432) Some of the music score from the cult 1988 movie Killer Klowns from Outer Space can be heard when Dustin's toys come to life in the first episode of Stranger

Things 3.

(433) Stranger Things 2 takes place during an election. Ted Wheeler has a Ronald Reagan placard in his garden. Dustin's mother is clearly a Democrat as she has a Walter Mondale placard.

(434) Lucas has a crush on Nancy in the pilot script for Stranger Things. In the actual show they made Dustin the one who has a crush on Nancy.

(435) Ross Duffer has said that he and his brother do worry about the sudden fame the show bestowed on the younger Stranger Things cast members but think they have coped with it well and so far remained grounded.

(436) Millie Bobby Brown said the kids on Stranger Things often play board games between takes.

(437) In 2020, Gaten joined forces with Happy Socks on a collection to celebrate the holidays called No Time Like the Present.

(438) The most impenetrable reference in Stranger Things 2 comes when Dustin is on the telephone to Mr McCorkle. Mr McCorkle was the name of a neighbour the Duffers had when they were kids.

(439) Some fans thought that Dustin secretly adopting Dart in Stranger Things 2 was decidedly out of character because Dustin was the most logical and sensible of the boys in season one. It seems odd that Dustin appears blind to the obvious dangers of adopting a creature from the Upside Down.

(440) Gaten enjoys pastries.

(441) Gaten says that the travel involved in being an actor is tough but all part of the job.

(442) Gaten is a big fan of the TV show Orange is the New Black.

(443) Gaten supports the New York Knicks basketball team.

(444) The kids in Stranger Things all have their own stunt doubles.

(445) Gaten enjoys a raspberry mocktail. This is a non-alcoholic drink.

(446) Gaten said that when he was younger he was sometimes teased about his cleidocranial dysplasia by other kids but this made him a stronger person in the end.

(447) There's a YouTube video of an eleven year-old Gaten giving a backstage tour for a performance of Les Misérables on Broadway.

(448) Finn Wolfhard said he was surprised by how good Gaten's singing voice was during the NeverEnding Story duet in Stranger Things 3.

(449) Gaten's fashion style has been described as smart casual.

(450) Gaten says that him and Stranger Things co-star Joe Keery are friends off screen too.

(451) Gaten doesn't seem to have jumped into movies in

the same way that other Stranger Things cast members have. Millie Bobby Brown, Finn Wolfhard, and David Harbour have all made a number of movies off the back of Stranger Things.

(452) The Stranger Things kids bonded by going to amusement parks together.

(453) Gaten is famous for his distinctive laugh.

(454) Gaten has taken part in video game sessions on Twitch for charity.

(455) Gaten says it is important not to become obsessed with fame and celebrity and tries to live as normal life as possible away from the camera.

(456) The overnight fame the tremendous success of Stranger Things bestowed on the cast (save for Winona Ryder - who was plenty famous already) took them all by surprise. Gaten said it was very surreal to be recognised in the street after Stranger Things was a big hit in 2016.

(457) Gaten said the first script he had for Stranger Things (or Montauk as it would have been called at the time) gave no inkling of how good the show would actually turn out to be.

(458) Stranger Things was rejected by many networks before it ended up on Netflix.

(459) Gaten's show Prank Encounters is basically a modern version of Candid Camera. The twist is that the pranks have a supernatural or fantastical twist.

(460) Gaten seems to have longer hair than usual in

Stranger Things 4.

(461) Gaten is a big fan of Central Park in New York.

(462) Gaten said he would love to have a cameo as a Stormtrooper in Star Wars.

(463) Gaten is a fan of potato chips.

(464) Despite his tender years, Gaten is already something of a talk show veteran.

(465) Gaten seems to be a very down to earth chap. There are no stories of him going on lavish spending sprees or living a party lifestyle.

(466) The Duffers double downed on the chemistry between Gaten and Joe Keery by teaming Steve with Dustin again in Stranger Things 3.

(467) Gaten says he has a lot of the curiosity of Dustin Henderson and tended to ask his teachers a lot of questions.

(468) Gaten is a fan of The Walking Dead.

(469) The eagle eyed bike enthusiasts who watched Stranger Things were confused why the lights on the boys bikes seemed to be orange during daylight sequences in season one. Orange lights were not used on bikes in the eighties. The mystery was solved when it was deduced that the orange 'lights' were orange gels. They were used by the production designers so the bike lights could be altered to match the production lights at night and no undesired hues could occur.

(470) The boys in Stranger Things owe a certain debt to the kids in The Goonies as they bicker, swear, and undertake a dangerous quest. Barb's spectacles in Stranger Things are a probable nod to Martha Plimpton in The Goonies, and Dustin clearly owes something to 'Chunk'.

(471) The extras hired for the Snow Ball scenes in Stranger Things 2 were not told at first that they had been hired for Stranger Things. They soon worked it out though.

(472) The scenes in season one of Stranger Things where the boys walk the train tracks was shot at Stone Mountain Park.

(473) Practically every character in Stranger Things wears corduroy at some point!

(474) Gaten campaigns for cleidocranial dysplasia to be regarded as a medical rather than dental condition because he believes those with the condition should be covered by medical insurance.

(475) Gaten says he would like to end his career in the theatre because that's where it all began for him.

(476) Gaten says his cats have a habit of following him into the bathroom and shower!

(477) According to babycenter.com, Gaten was the 11,388th most popular boy's name in 2018. If these statistics are right it must be a very rare and unusual name!

(478) In the scenes in Stranger Things where the

characters are talking on walkie-talkies, the dialogue coming through the walkie-talkies is spoken to the actor on the set so they can react in a natural way.

(479) Peyton Wich, who played the odious school bully Troy in season one of Stranger Things, said that Gaten and the kids were so nice in real life that it was difficult sometimes to get into character as Troy and be mean to them.

(480) In season two of Stranger Things, Mike explains the roles his gang have in Dungeons & Dragons terms. Mike is the Paladin, Dustin the Bard, Will the stealthy Rogue, Lucas the Ranger, and Eleven the Magician.

(481) David Harbour said he did some method acting at the start of season one of Stranger Things. When production started, he was deliberately aloof and kept his distance from the children for a time to get into the character of the grouchy Hopper.

(482) Stranger Things fashion designer Kim Wilcox said the fashion of the individual boys at the Snow Ball dance is a hint to their futures. Dustin is wearing a bow tie. Might that mean an academic future lies ahead for Dustin?

(483) Stranger Things was launched on Netflix on July 15, 2016.

(484) HP Lovecraft was an inspiration for Stranger Things. Lovecraft was a horror author who imagined a universe full of inexplicable creatures, dimensions and entities that can't be explained.

(485) Spielberg's 1982 film E.T is the single biggest

source for homages in Stranger Things. The story of a boy who bonds with a stranded alien and gives it refuge has some obvious parallels with the way Mike gives Eleven sanctuary and develops a bond with her. In episode four the boys even disguise Eleven in a wig and dress - just like the kids do to the alien in E.T.

(486) Dustin in described in the Stranger Things 'pitch bible' in the following way - 'Dustin Henderson, twelve, is the "King Geek." He is overweight and wears oversized glasses. His supportive parents are nerds themselves and are supportive of his choices and hobbies. However, Dustin finds less acceptance at school, where he is often bullied for his weight and interests. He frequently bickers with Lucas; their arguments are good-natured at first, but escalate as the stakes rise.'

(487) The timeline in Stranger Things has the kids in Stranger Things 3 (set in 1985) about to begin their freshman year of high school.

(488) Canada was the country where the first season of Stranger Things went viral the fastest.

(489) Dart eating Dustin's cat Mews in Stranger Things 2 is a possible reference to the eighties sitcom ALF - about a cuddly extraterrestrial who lived with a family on Earth and was always threatening to eat the cat.

(490) Gaten enjoys visiting his local Biggby Coffee.

(491) Gaten supports the New York Rangers hockey team.

(492) Gaten said that like most teenagers he would probably go loopy if he was separated from his phone for a prolonged period of time.

(493) The kids in Stranger Things say that Gaten is the biggest prankster on the set. He would dispute this.

(494) Walkie-talkies were popular with kids in the eighties, even if they were just talking to each other in the same house from upstairs. They were fun to use.

(495) A Stranger Things Monopoly game was released by Hasbro.

(496) Stranger Things was a genuine word of mouth phenomenon. The first season did not have a huge amount of publicity or promotion but positive reviews encouraged viewers to seek it out.

(497) Dustin's pet creature Dart was complex to design because Dart had to go through four stages of development from slug to Deomodog.

(498) Teaming up Steve with Dustin in Stranger Things 2 was not something that was planned from the start. They only had this idea two or three episodes into shooting.

(499) The cannisters of green gloop that Steve and Dustin find in Stranger Things 3 are similar to the big canister of green liquid the students in John Carpenter's Prince of Darkness find.

(500) The arcade game with cartoon animation that Dustin and boys seem both enchanted and frustrated with in equal measure in Stranger Things 2 is called Dragon's Lair. This was an unusual game that came out in 1983. It featured animation by a former Disney animator named Don Bluth and was more of a choose your fate adventure than an arcade game. The player made a choice and then

watched the next animation play out to see if they had made the right choice or the wrong choice. Dragon's Lair was popular at first but this type of game didn't catch on. Watching the game's hero hero Dirk the Daring get killed in cartoon animation simply became annoying (and expensive) for players.

(501) Gaten said he would like to visit Belgium.

(502) Gaten has English, Finnish, Scottish, German, and Irish ancestry on his mother's side.

(503) The surname Matarazzo is typical of an Italian family name in Campania.

(504) Gaten grew up in Mystic Village.

(505) Gaten is a big fan of the film Deadpool.

(506) Gaten can play the piano.

(507) Gaten says he prefers watching sports to playing them.

(508) Gaten likes Marmite. Marmite is a food spread made from yeast extract.

(509) Gaten is known as 'Gate' to the other Stranger Things cast members.

(510) At 2010 US tennis open, Gaten sang America the Beautiful. He was only seven at the time.

(511) Gaten's brother Carmen plays the drums in Gaten's band Work in Progress.

(512) Gaten has been nominated for a IGN Summer Movie Award for his work in Stranger Things.

(513) Gaten says he enjoys reading to relax when he has the time.

(514) Gaten said that when Stranger Things first became available to stream on Netflix in 2016 he had a special binge party with his family to celebrate. He said he was the only person who made it through all eight episodes without falling asleep!

(515) Gaten said he related to the character of the doomed Barb Holland in the first season of Stranger Things.

(516) Gaten doesn't speak Italian.

(517) The Stranger Things kids famously performed Uptown Funk at the Emmys.

(518) Gaten says he likes country music.

(519) Gaten appeared in a school production of The 25th Annual Putnam County Spelling Bee. The 25th Annual Putnam County Spelling Bee is a musical comedy.

(520) Gaten can read sheet music.

(521) Gaten says he doesn't like it when fans take sneak photographs of him from a distance or through a window. He would prefer they just come and talk to him.

(522) Gaten is a big fan of the Rodgers and Hammerstein musical Oklahoma!

(523) Gaten says that social media feels like a chore and

he only really uses it because it is part of his job.

(524) Gaten said he did Prank Encounters because it was an opportunity to do something new and different.

(525) Gaten's extended family have a big weekly dinner date together.

(526) Gaten joined Twitter in 2015.

(527) In 2020, Gaten underwent a surgery which removed fourteen supernumerary teeth that would allow his adult teeth to come through.

(528) Gaten said that before he got his breaks with The Blacklist and Stranger Things he would go to about three auditions a week and experience constant rejections. This is pretty standard for jobbing actors though. It can be a very tough business.

(529) In 2019, Gaten attended a Stranger Things Netflix party in Rome.

(530) Gaten said he celebrated Stranger Things getting a second season by going to Starbucks.

(531) The school in Stranger Things is a real school in Georgia that closed in 2015 because of a mould infestation.

(532) The Duffers said that Gaten was such a charismatic scene stealer in season one of Stranger Things that it was a no brainer to expand the part of Dustin Henderson in season two.

(533) Gaten said that life in his Italian family is hectic and

crazy but a lot of fun too.

(534) The props department and set decorators had to find a lot of vintage (and sometimes defunct) brands to populate the backdrops in Stranger Things. Everything you see in the background in season one, be it washing powder, coffee, beer, potato chips, or soda, had to seem authentic to 1983.

(535) The scene where in the season one finale of Stranger Things where Dustin finds the school stash of Hunt's Snack Pack chocolate puddings in the finale was a clever piece of improvisation by the props team. In 1983 these puddings still came in metal tins and only changed to plastic cups in 1984. The props department therefore purchased some metal tins of luncheon meat and stuck Hunt's Snack Pack chocolate pudding labels on them.

(536) The children in Stranger Things liken the Upside Down to the Plane of Shadows. The Plane of Shadows is a dimension that exists alongside our own reality. It is there all the time in close proximity but elusive. Although the Duffers are vague about the true nature of the Upside Down we see that actions in our own reality can have a ripple effect in this mysterious Nether.

(537) A number of actors (including Gaten) in Stranger Things have said that Duffer Brothers allow them to have a lot of input into the evolution of their characters.

(538) On the unavoidable delay to Stranger Things 4 due to the pandemic, Gaten said that it was a blessing in disguise because it allowed more time for the scripts to be refined and completed.

(539) Dustin and Suzie singing The Neverending Story

song in Stranger Things 3 became something of a mixed blessing for the crew because the kids couldn't stop singing it for days afterwards and it became an 'earworm' for everyone in the production.

(540) Generous tax incentives in Georgia for screen productions was a factor in why Atlanta was chosen as the production base for Stranger Things.

(541) Gaten and the boys said they got fed up wearing shorts in Stranger Things 3. They had to though because that season was set in the summer.

(542) The first season of Stranger Things required around 150 wigs for the cast and extras. Gaten's hair was his own though.

(543) A survey in 2017 found 31% of young adults had watched all the episodes of Stranger Things.

(544) Natalia Dyer (who plays Nancy Wheeler) said she worries about the fame the younger cast members in Stranger Things had to cope with but thinks they have handled it well.

(545) A comic called Stranger Things - Zombie Boys has the boys making a horror movie for Halloween. The comic is set between seasons one and two.

(546) In season one of Stranger Things, the school bully Troy calls Dustin's gang losers. This is a reference to the loser's club in Stephen King's IT.

(547) The scripts on Stranger Things are quite fluid in that the Duffers like to give themselves enough flexibility to change plot points - even during production. This is

why the actors in the show never seem to be completely sure what is actually going to happen in any given season.

(548) For the first ever scene in Stranger Things the Duffers put the boys in the Wheeler basement set for hours to shoot the Dungeons & Dragons game that begins the show. This was a shrewd way to make the boys bond quickly.

(549) Millie Bobby Brown said the Stranger Things kids never talk about dating.

(550) Although Millie Bobby Brown was separate from Gaten and the boys for most of Stranger Things season two in her scenes as Eleven, she saw them on the set all the time because they had their school classes together during the production.

(551) Winona Ryder was bewildered on the set of Stranger Things when Gaten and the kids started talking about Snapchat. She thought Snapchat was a cafe.

(552) The kids have some Yoo-hoo drinks in Stranger Things 3. Yoo-hoo is a brand of chocolate beverage that was developed by Natale Olivieri in Garfield, New Jersey in 1928.

(553) Of the four boys in Stranger Things, Millie Bobby Brown said - "The boys have their squads. They have their group, and it's definitely difficult because they're boys and talk about boy stuff. They talk about girls and video games. I definitely need to talk about normal things a girl would talk about. They're like my big brothers. They annoy me, but we are very, very close."

(554) It takes about two or three weeks to shoot an

episode of Stranger Things. The special effects obviously take a lot longer than this to complete though.

(555) The Duffer Brothers said it was a great relief when they started shooting Stranger Things and saw the children were all excellent actors with good chemistry. As they pointed out, one bad performance from one of the children could have sunk the entire show!

(556) Gaten said that, between production, he sometimes goes weeks and months without seeing his Stranger Things co-stars but they instantly slide back into their friendships when they meet up again.

(557) Waitresses at the Stranger Things 2 premiere were dressed in special Eggo yellow uniforms.

(558) The fame of Stranger Things is such that it was the subject of a jovial Sesame Street parody in 2017.

(559) Gaten thinks Stranger Things is popular because the outcasts and outsiders are the heroes in the show.

(560) Universal Studios Hollywood created some Stranger Things themed treats to mark Halloween in 2019. These included Eleven's Waffle Sundae.

(561) The Duffers didn't want 'Disney' kids when they were casting Stranger Things. They wanted to avoid child actors who seemed too arch, too showy, or too aware of the camera. They wanted kids who seemed authentic and felt like real children.

(562) Millie Bobby Brown said that the kids on Stranger Things are always stealing one another's potato chips on the set.

(563) The first full trailer for Stranger Things 3 had 22 million views in one week on YouTube.

(564) The first season of Stranger Things was produced in relative obscurity. There wasn't much buzz about the show and aside from Winona Ryder and Matthew Modine no one had heard of most of the cast. That all changed when they started shooting Stranger Things 2. Overheard drones buzzed the set trying to capture footage and Gaten and the kids were now famous around the world.

(565) Stranger Things producer Shawn Levy said that when you cast child actors you audition the families as much as you audition the kids. He said they prefer to cast kids who have supportive and grounded relatives.

(566) One theory for why the Duffers got over a dozen rejections when they first tried to pitch Stranger Things is that there had been a number of underwhelming television shows and miniseries based on the stories of Stephen King. The prospect of another show heavily inspired by Stephen King evidently wasn't an appealing prospect to many executives.

(567) Stranger Things casting director Carmen Cuba said - "Training and/or life experience teaches adults how to leave some of their quirks off the table. But kids are mostly unable to cover up the things that make them uniquely who they are — and I love that."

(568) Gaten is pretty familiar and at home in Atlanta now after shooting four seasons of Stranger Things there.

(569) Gaten says that Stranger Things 4 is his favourite season when it comes to the clothes and costumes that

Dustin Henderson has to wear.

(570) Gaten said that his favourite episode of Prank Encounters is the one with Bigfoot.

(571) Gaten said it was pretty amazing to have his likeness turned into a Stranger Things action figure.

(572) Gaten said he enjoys voice acting because recording studios are usually very plush and comfortable places to hang around.

(573) Gaten says that one of the best things about working on Stranger Things is the food. The catering is very good.

(574) Gaten said he would love to be in a big movie one day. Gaten said he ended up discussing 80s movies a lot at his Stranger Things auditions. The other kids in the cast said this happened to them too.

(575) Gaten says that theatre has an exciting edge to it because everything is live and you can't do another take if you fluff a scene.

(576) Gaten said that for some of his commercials he was allowed to improvise and shoot his own contribution on his phone.

(577) Although they do a lot of covers, Gaten's band Work in Progress have released some original songs.

(578) Gaten helps write the lyrics for the songs Work in Progress have released.

(579) Gaten said it was fun to see the Stranger Things sets

for the first time and look at all the 1980s props.

(580) Gaten seems to be a big fan of coca-cola.

(581) Gaten thinks that Dustin Henderson is much cleverer and more academic than he is in real life.

(582) Gaten says that when a new season of Stranger Things comes out he finds he is recognised a lot more in his day to day life but in the hiatus between seasons his level of fame dies down somewhat.

(583) Gaten said he was a bit disappointed that they didn't get to shoot any school scenes for Stranger Things 3. He said he loves the school set.

(584) Gaten said that Millie Bobby Brown has pranked him a few times by pretending to be a fan on the telephone.

(585) Gaten said he would hate to wear a wig on Stranger Things because they are itchy and uncomfortable. He much prefers to just grow his hair out.

(586) Gaten is a fan of cotton candy.

(587) Gaten is a fan of pancakes.

(588) Gaten said that going back to make Starnger Things 2 was like a family reunion.

(589) Gaten tends to greet fans on social media by saying 'You dudes!'

(590) Gaten's personal t-shirt design for his cleidocranial dysplasia charity had a Ghostbusters theme.

(591) Gaten said it was a strange experience to learn that one fan had got a Dustin Henderson Stranger Things tattoo in tribute to the character!

(592) Gaten says he often has an omelette if he's eating breakfast in a diner.

(593) Although it is sometimes suggested that the first season of Stranger Things operated on a modest budget this is not really true. At $6 million an episode, the first season cost around $50 million. While this is modest compared to big Hollywood movie blockbusters, $6 million an episode is fairly high end for a TV show - especially a brand new one with no track record to speak of.

(594) Steven Spielberg has praised Stranger Things and said he enjoys the show.

(595) The bikes that the boys ride in Stranger Things are not specific makes but mash-ups using different props and parts to make them look like eighties bikes. This was because the actors had to have extra bikes (in case of damage) and it was too difficult to find that many identical bikes from the eighties.

(596) The Duffers chose distinct subgenres for the age groups in season one of Stranger Things. The teenage characters are in a classic horror film like Halloween or A Nightmare On Elm Street. The child characters are in an adventure like The Goonies or The Monster Squad. The adult characters are in a mystery like Close Encounters of the Third Kind or Invasion of the Body Snatchers.

(597) Gaten's band were on the cover of The Aquarian

Weekly magazine.

(598) Gaten is left-handed.

(599) Gaten is a fan of breadsticks.

(600) Time Magazine listed Gaten as one of the 30 most influential teens of 2016.

(601) Gaten's siblings have both been in TV commercials.

(602) Fancasting sites think Gaten would make a good Samwise Gamgee in The Lord of the Rings.

(603) The Duffers say that most of the networks who rejected Stranger Things wanted it to be more like Twin Peaks.

(604) A demographic breakdown for Stranger Things showed it was very popular with females as women and girls accounted for 57% of the audience.

(605) You can now buy a Funko Pop Demogorgon toy.

(606) For New York comic con, twenty Dustin Henderson lookalikes on pedicabs were dispatched to the streets blasting eighties music.

(607) You see some Hostess Filled Sno-Balls in the Stranger Things season three episode The Flayed. Sno Balls are cream-filled chocolate cakes covered with marshmallow frosting and coconut flakes.

(608) A Stranger Things Pez dispenser line was released in 2018. Dustin and Lucas feature on the dispensers.

(609) Limahl's NeverEnding Story song experienced an 800% increase in streams after Stranger Things 3 came out.

(610) The most pressing task for the production team on Stranger Things 3 was the creation of the Starcourt Mall that would feature so prominently in the story. It was obviously not feasible to build a gigantic mall sized set in a studio and the solution turned out to be Gwinnett Place Mall - an abandoned and derelict mall that sat on the outskirts of Atlanta. Gwinnett Place Mall was first operational in 1984 but had been empty and closed for a few years when the Stranger Things team found it. In 2017, the dead body of a murdered woman was found in the mall - such was its dilapidated and forgotten condition. The mall was in a complete state of disrepair but it did have two levels and plenty of space for cameras and a production crew to shoot in. The building had vast potential if it could be cleaned up and decorated. Netflix leased about 20% of the mall in the end to use for Stranger Things 3.

(611) Stranger Things production designer Chris Trujillo and a team of eighty people spent six weeks renovating Gwinnett Place Mall by restoring the facades and signs, cleaning the place up, adding lights, and putting in operational stores and a food court. Trujillo worked in malls when he was a teenager and used his own memories of being a 'mallrat' to bring Starcourt Mall to life. The end results were astonishing and the actors were amazed when they saw Starcourt Mall for the first time. Trujillo and his team had taken a bleak abandoned building and turned it into something that genuinely looked and felt like a real functioning 1980s mall.

(612) Dustin's cymbal-clapping monkey toy that comes to

life (thanks to Eleven) in Stranger Things 3 could be a reference to the Stephen King story The Monkey.

(613) Stranger Things products now available include a 'Where's Barb?' book and an Upside Down Snow Globe.

(614) At the Stranger Things 2 premiere, the Hawkins Fair themed party served corn dogs, funnel cakes, fresh donuts, and cocktails such as the UpCider Down, the Maple Bourbon Bone Chiller, and Pumpkin Ale.

(615) The design of the Upside Down in Stranger Things was made easier by everyone involved in the production design and special effects having a similar concept of what it should look like. They all saw this as a place of vines and spores and a landscape that appeared ravaged by disease. They wanted the Upside Down to look wet and swampy and be a murky and misty place to explore. The inspirations for the Upside Down are many and varied. Stephen King's The Mist (where a blanket of monster festooned fog descends on a town after a military experiment), was an obvious inspiration on both the Upside Down and the story in Stranger Things. The Phantom Zone prison dimension from the 1984 film Supergirl and the ghostly mist engulfed town of Silent Hill in the video game and movie series were also influences on the Upside Down.

Other inspirations for the Upside Down were the nightmare planet LV-426 in Ridley Scott's Alien and James Cameron's Aliens (you could equally mention Planet of the Vampires aka errore nello spazio - a 1965 Mario Bava gothic space opera that Alien was heavily influenced by), the 'Zone' (a restricted area of great mystery) in the 1979 science fiction film Stalker by Andrei Tarkovsky, the fog smoked hell dimension of spooky decayed corridors the Cenobites in Clive Barker's Hellraiser inhabit, the dark imagery and immersive sound design of the video game Dark Souls, the baroque paintings of Zdzislaw Beksinski, Xen (the strange Borderworld connecting dimensions in the Half-Life video games), the Hellmouths' from Buffy the Vampire Slayer, the desolate planet Luminos in the Outer Limits episode A Feasibility Study, and the bank of thick supernatural mist that heralds the arrival of the zombie pirates in John Carpenter's The Fog.

The Upside Down scenes in season one Stranger Things were enhanced by digital spores and strange sound effects. The sound department added disconcerting creaks and groans and made the score for Upside Down scenes ambient and unsettling.

(616) One of the most entertaining if improbable Stranger Things fan theories is that the Mind Flayer in season two is an evil manifestation of Barb Holland bent on revenge against Hawkins.

(617) Gaten has something in common with his Stranger Things co-star Joe Keery because Joe has been in some music bands.

(618) Gaten said that Green Day was one of the first bands he ever saw in concert.

(619) Gaten and Joe Keery seemed to have matched their looks at the 20189 Sage Awards. They both had slicked back hair and black outfits.

(620) The credits in the Stranger Things opening title sequence are designed to look like a puzzle that is slowly coming together.

(621) The sequence where the kids and teenagers hide from the monster in the Gap store in Stranger Things 3 is inspired by a sequence in the Steven Spielberg film version of The War of the Worlds.

(622) Gaten is a fan of Jaguar cars.

(623) Gaten has recorded promotional videos for his beloved New York Rangers.

(624) In April 2021, Gaten got his second dose of the pandemic vaccine and took to Instagram imploring everyone to get vaccinated.

(625) You can now buy a Gaten Matarazzo throw pillow.

(626) The boys (Finn, Lucas, Gaten) in Stranger Things say they want Nancy to end up with Jonathan ('Jancy') while Millie Bobby Brown prefers 'Stancy' and wants Nancy to be with Steve.

(627) In Stranger Things 2, we see that Dustin has a Wheel of Fortune board game in his house.

(628) The first teaser trailer for Stranger Things 2 featured a real 1980 Eggo commercial featuring (future) Wonder Years star Jason Hervey.

(629) Gaten is a fan of 80s band The Smiths.

(630) Gaten had to travel between New Jersey and New York City a lot when he was on Broadway.

(631) Gaten is a big fan of breakfast cereal.

(632) Stranger Things takes place in Roane County. This county doesn't really exist in Indiana.

(633) Gaten is quite rare in the Stranger Things cast in that he loves horror movies in real life. Sadie Sink, Natalia Dyer, Charlie Heaton, and Priah Ferguson have all said they are not horror fans and don't watch horror shows or movies.

(634) Gaten is a fan of The Fratellis.

(635) Nike brought out some Cortez sneakers to mark season three of Stranger Things. The sneakers have the Russian code from season three that Dustin cracks printed on them.

(636) Shawn Levy said the Scoop Troop (the team of Steve, Robin, Erica, and Dustin) in Stranger Things 3 was not something that was planned in advance but an idea they had as production was gearing up. The Duffers like the idea of throwing in team-ups that you might not have expected and Steve becoming part of a team with Erica Sinclair was such a crazy idea they couldn't resist implementing it

(637) George Romero's Day of the Dead is the film that Dustin and the kids (thanks to Steve) smuggle themselves in the Starcourt cinema to watch in the first episode of Stranger Things 3. Day of the Dead was unrated because of its many gore scenes and so the young teenagers wouldn't have been able to buy a ticket themselves. The film hadn't actually been released yet when Stranger Things 3 is set but it is just about possible that Starcourt managed to obtain a preview screening.

(638) Gaten seems to be a fan of colourful socks.

(639) All the members of Gaten's band Work in Progress went to the same school.

(640) Gaten is a fan of Billy Joel.

(641) The candy store It'Sugar introduced some Stranger Things goodies to celebrate the show. These included Gummy Eggos, Erica's Sugar Justice Box, and character themed lollipops.

(642) At the end of Stranger Things 2, we saw Dustin put a DemoDog in the fridge to preserve it as scientific evidence. However, Stranger Things 3 does not tie up this loose end. There is no mention in season three of what happened to the DemoDog in the fridge. It seems very likely that the Duffers included this scene in Stranger Things 2 as something that would have future consequences in season three but then changed their mind and decided not to follow through with the ramifications of this. As a consequence, the DemoDog in the fridge is completely forgotten in Stranger Things 3. Maybe the Duffer Brothers just forgot about the DemoDog!

(643) In the second episode of Stranger Things 2, Dustin wears a Casio F-91W digital watch. These were only available from 1991 so you could classify this as a mild goof because Stranger Things 2 is set in 1984.

(644) A DVD release of season one of Stranger Things by Target was designed so that the DVD case looked like a faded VHS tape.

(645) Maurice Jarre's score from Peter Weir's 1985 film Witness is used during the radio tower scenes with Dustin

in Stranger Things 3.

(646) The Duffers say that the fact the children in the cast grew up fast is good because it means Stranger Things will feel different each time it returns.

(647) Gaten was featured on the cover of the February 2019 edition of Media Planet magazine.

(648) The problem with Stranger Things comics so far is that none of them feel especially ambitious and the art leaves something to be desired. Most of these comics seemed aimed squarely at kids whereas the TV show is watched by people of all ages. We will probably have to wait for Stranger Things to end before we get a really good comic that can use the full mythology of the show.

(649) Gaten said that Qui-Gon is the character from Star Wars he would most like to have dinner with.

(650) Gaten is a fan of Bob Dylan.

(651) Gaten attended the Star Wars: The Rise of Skywalker Premiere in LA.

(652) In 2020, Gaten appeared in a musical theatre parody of Star Wars for charity.

(653) Gaten wore an #ASOS Skinny Crop Blazer in neon yellow to the Stranger Things 3 premiere.

(654) Gaten wore a Gucci tux at the Emmys.

(655) At the SAG Awards in 2020, Gaten wore a velvet plaid tuxedo shaded midnight blue by Strong Suit.

(656) Gaten tried some Irn Bru for a YouTube video and said he liked it. Irn Bru is a famous Scottish fizzy soft drink.

(657) The Duffers auditioned 906 boys and 307 girls before deciding on their younger cast members in Stranger Things.

(658) Gaten is a fan of the vintage band Toto.

(659) Hugh Everett III (1930 – 1982) was the creator of the Many-Worlds Interpretation (MWI) of quantum mechanics, a.k.a. the Everett Interpretation. Everett proposed a multiverse where anything that could happen will have occurred in some alternate universe. Mr Clarke, the science teacher in Stranger Things, mentions Everett's thesis when Dustin and the boys ask him about alternate dimensions.

(660) Dustin's band has performed at The Troubadour in Los Angeles.

(661) The use of other dimensions or alternate realities in fictional entertainment is not exactly a new idea. Everyone from Lovecraft to Stephen King has used this device in stories. Dimensions, portals, and alternate realities have long been a staple of comics, movies, and anthology shows like The Twilight Zone and The Outer Limits. It is to the credit of the Duffers that they took something we were already familiar with (too familiar you might argue) but still managed to make it feel fresh, intriguing, and mysterious in Stranger Things.

(662) Shawn Levy, the producer of Stranger Things, believes that the Duffers got so many initial rejections because no one thought that a show based around kids

would work. Anyone who thought Stranger Things would be improved by removing all the children clearly didn't really understand what the Duffers were doing at all!

(663) In Dungeons & Dragons, thessalmonsters are a group of related creatures designed to resemble the hydra. The thessalhydra first appeared in first edition in the original Monster Manual II. The creature features in the boys' Dungeons & Dragons game in episode eight of season one of Stranger Things. This anticipates the hydra-like Mind Flayer in season two.

(664) Dustin Henderson lives with his doting mother and has a vast mastery of pop culture trivia at his disposal to make the situations faced by the boys in Stranger Things more readily explainable to his friends (and the audience watching at home).

(665) Pyramid Head, a creature in Silent Hill with no face, was a big inspiration for the look of the Demogorgon in season one of Stranger Things

(666) Gaten is a fan of REM.

(667) When Dustin is trying to get hold of Lucas on his walkie-talkie because of the Dart crisis in Stranger Things 2 and gets the brush off from Erica, Erica is stealing a He-Man toy from Lucas' bedroom. He-Man and the Masters of the Universe was a cartoon that ran on television from 1983 until 1985.

(668) A Funko Pop signed by Gaten usually sells for about $150.

(669) In these days of information overload, angry social media, 24 hours news, and ubiquitous cell phones, who

doesn't sometimes yearn to be transported back to a simpler time? As Gaten has said, perhaps this is one of the many charms of Stranger Things.

(670) The Palace Arcade in Stranger Things 2 has the popular machines Dragon's Lair, Dig Dug, Asteroids, Galaga, Centipede and Pac-Man. Kids in the early eighties could play video games at home on things like the Commodore 64 and Atari but they were rather rudimentary - at least in comparison to what came later. Home gaming made a quantum jump in the early and mid 1990s with games like Doom but that was the future as far as Stranger Things is concerned. For kids in the early eighties, the video game arcade was still a thing of wonder that offered them a gaming experience they couldn't get on their machines at home.

(671) There is a goof in Stranger Things 2 at the school because we see a periodic table with elements that hadn't been discovered yet in 1984. The elements in Mr Clarke's periodic table that weren't discovered yet include Darmstadtium (Ds), Roentgenium (Rg), Copernicium (Cn), Ununtrium (Uut), Flerovium (Fl), Ununpentium (Uup), Livermorium (Lv), Ununseptium (Uus) and Ununoctium (Uuo). Although - in contrast - the scientific t-shirt that Dustin wears in the arcade scenes does have correct 1970s elements.

(672) Gaten said he read the Stephen King book The Long Walk in only two days because he found it so gripping. The Long Walk is a dystopian horror novel published in 1979 under the pseudonym Richard Bachman.

(673) Gaten is a fan of Joss Stone.

(674) Dustin's band has performed at the Gas Monkey in

Dallas.

(675) Gaten says he likes all types of music and doesn't limit himself to any one genre.

(676) Gaten doesn't appear to have had any tattoos.

(677) Gaten often posts pictures of his girlfriend Lizzie Yu on Instagram.

(678) Gaten is a fan of the band Muse.

(679) Gaten says that if he can make someone laugh then that makes his day.

(680) Gaten thinks the difference between him and Dustin Henderson is that he is always trying to be funny whereas Dustin is funny without trying.

(681) Gaten said that - alas - he isn't a science whizz like Dustin Henderson.

(682) You can book Gaten for an appearance or speaking engagement through his management company. They do not disclose the fee though. I suppose you would have to actually book Gaten to know how it costs to hire him!

(683) Some of Gaten's fans think he would be a natural if he had his own sitcom.

(684) Gaten said he isn't sure what he'll do when Stranger Things ends but he's sure that something will turn up in the end.

(685) Gaten thinks that social media has the potential to be dangerous because it can lower one's self-esteem.

(686) Though they are often much maligned, Gaten enjoys the Star Wars prequels.

(687) Gaten thinks that Millie Bobby Brown would be good on Broadway because she's a natural diva.

(688) Gaten said he only knew for sure that Hopper would be in Stranger Things 4 when he saw David Harbour at the table read for the new season.

(689) Gaten is a fan of the old Gwen Stefani band No Doubt.

(690) Gaten said that Stranger Things 4 is the scariest season yet.

(691) In 2017, Joe Keery said of working with Gaten in Stranger Things - "I've primarily worked with actors the same age as me for the past four years, so working with somebody who is 10 years younger than me, you learn a whole different set of skills."

(692) Gaten received many messages of support from the Stranger Things cast during his surgeries for Cleidocranial Dysplasia.

(693) Gaten says he misses the other Stranger Things kids when a season is not in production and they are all miles apart.

(694) Gaten said his message to those with Cleidocranial Dysplasia is to stay positive.

(695) Asked what he's scared of, Gaten said that being the last person left alive in a zombie outbreak would be pretty

terrifying!

(696) Gaten said that on Stranger Things they were supplied with authentic 1980s underwear by the costume department but he realised at some point he was the only cast member who was actually wearing it!

(697) In response to being asked if he has stolen anything from the set of Stranger Things, Gaten said the only thing he takes is food.

(698) Gaten said he was one of those rare kids who loved school and didn't see it as a chore.

(699) Gaten said that when he became famous he didn't talk about Stranger Things much with his friends because it was nice to get away from the show and just be a normal person.

(700) Sadly, although the mall set and stores stayed in place for several months after shooting on Stranger Things 3 ended, Netflix eventually dismantled the Starcourt Mall set and stores and took everything away. The main reason for this was the high cost of maintaining full time security measures and staff to stop fans sneaking into the mall and taking props as souvenirs. Some local people connected to the mall wanted the Starcourt sets to stay in place and become a permanent tourist attraction and it seems a shame that this didn't happen. Who wouldn't want to do some shopping at the Starcourt Mall? It is believed that Netflix decided to dismantle things like the Scoops Ahoy props and shop for future use in a theme park. They ended up removing everything else too. Gwinnett Place Mall was put up for sale again after all the props and sets were removed and its future remains uncertain. There has been talk of some business people

wanting to turn the site into a sports stadium.

(701) The Upside Down was called the Nether in the original Stranger Things scripts.

(702) The special effects on season one were only completed days before Stranger Things was due to begin streaming on Netflix.

(703) When the first season of Stranger Things came out, Gaten described his character Dustin as a gregarious, foul-mouthed 12-year-old boy.

(704) Gaten said he wasn't commanding enough for the part of Mike Wheeler and was much more suited to playing the quirkier Dustin Henderson.

(705) Gaten said that out of the first season of Stranger Things he liked the finale the best because that's when all the crazy stuff happened.

(706) Gaten said he used to make little home movies when he was a kid.

(707) Loch Nora, where the kids go trick or treating in Stranger Things 2, is the name of a real place near where the Duffer Brothers grew up in North Carolina.

(708) Steve and Dustin leave a trail of meat in the woods to lure Dart in Stranger Things 2. Watermelon was used to depict the meat in these scenes because of its vibrant red colour.

(709) When the DemoDogs sneak up on Steve and Dustin at the junkyard in Stranger Things 2, this is a homage to Bob Peck's game warden being surprised by the

Velociraptor in Jurassic Park.

(710) Stranger Things was shot on a digital cinema camera but to achieve the vintage look a layer of scanned film grain was added to the colouring process.

(711) Stranger Things reminded some readers of Dan Simmons' 1991 novel Summer of Night. Summer of Night takes place in a small Illinois town in 1960 and revolves around a gang of boys who are around twelve years-old. The boys love riding their bikes and making dens in the woods. They gradually realise that some mysterious evil has awoken in their town.

(712) Limahl had never heard of Stranger Things before they used his Neverending Story song in the Stranger Things 3 finale.

(713) The Duffer Brothers have said that the 2011 JJ Abrams film Super 8 was an influence on Stranger Things. Super 8 is set in the late 1970s and has a gang of children investigating a strange mystery in their small town.

(714) 13% of former Netflix subscribers rejoined the streaming platform specifically to watch Stranger Things 3.

(715) Pez is an Austrian candy which comes in a dispenser.

(716) Gaten said that one of his biggest fears is becoming disconnected from his old friends because of his work.

(717) The Cross Brothers of alt-pop band Computer Games said they wrote the music video treatment for Lost

Boys Life with Gaten in mind so it was a great relief when he agreed to appear in it.

(718) Gaten says he enjoys making Prank Encounters because it's very unpredictable. You never know what is going to happen.

(719) When it comes to 80s music, Gaten thinks that Dustin Henderson would be into Duran Duran or New Order.

(720) The first season of Stranger Things has a plot that is rather similar to a Twilight Zone episode called Little Girl Lost. Little Girl Lost is about a girl who becomes trapped in an alternate dimension thanks to a portal in her bedroom.

(721) Gaten visited Rome, Naples, and Capri when he went to Italy.

(722) Gaten said he would love to do some experimental theatre.

(723) When he went to Finland, Gaten visited Ivalo.

(724) Gaten said he would love to have powers of telekenisis like Eleven in Stranger Things.

(725) Gaten has appeared on Celebrity Family Feud. Celebrity Family Feud is a broadcast network spin-off of the syndicated American game show Family Feud.

(726) Gaten has appeared as a guest on Nickelodeon's Unfiltered.

(727) Gaten enjoys playing the guitar.

(728) To generate a spooky atmosphere on the set, the crew played the soundtrack to Close Encounters of the Third Kind during shooting on the junkyard sequence in Stranger Things 2.

(729) There was no official product placement in Stranger Things but the Kellogg Company in particular were delighted to see their stock price go up when Stranger Things came out because of the spike in demand for eggo waffles.

(730) After the first season of Stranger Things came out, a former employee at the Department of Energy wrote an article about the show and pointed out all the important and necessary tasks that the DOE does for the safety of the American public. The Duffers were very amused by this intervention. They thought it was funny that those connected to the DOE felt it necessary to inform the public that they were not involved in the development of super powered children or opening portals to other dimensions.

(731) The actors went their separate ways after the end of shooting on season one of Stranger Things and were uncertain if they'd ever be back or see each other again.

(732) In October, 2020, Gaten hosted State Theatre New Jersey's '80s Online Trivia Night.

(733) The place where Gaten worked as a food runner during the hiatus in production on Stranger Things 4 was Bird & Betty's on Long Beach Island .

(734) Most people thought that binging all eight episodes of Stranger Things in 2016 was much more fun than

watching the latest Hollywood blockbusters. Stranger Things was so good that even David Harbour said he binged the show and got all emotional when Will Byers was rescued at the end.

(735) Georgia International Horse Park was used for some of woodland scenes in season one of Stranger Things. This park hosted the equestrian competition in the 1996 Atlanta Olympics.

(736) A 2016 poll in Time Out named Hawkins in Stranger Things as the fictional place where people would most like to go on vacation. King's Landing and Hogwarts were second and third.

(737) The Stranger Things cast were allowed to do some free shopping at the Starcourt Mall near the end of shooting on season three. The expensive period authentic sneakers were off limits though because they were on loan.

(738) Noah Schnapp and Millie Bobby Brown have both confessed to taking home socks and underwear from the Stranger Things costume department. Gaten has never confessed to doing this tough.

(739) Many people thought it was a bit weird that Gaten took a summer job in a diner when has $4 million in the bank! Gaten said he simply wanted to do something constructive to kill time until production on Stranger Things began again.

(740) Bellwood Quarry in Georgia has been used not just for Stranger Things also The Walking Dead (which also has its production base in Georgia).

(741) The junkyard sequence in Stranger Things 2 was shot in a real junkyard.

(742) The main production base of Stranger Things is the 10-stage, 33-acre EUE Screen Gems Studios in Atlanta.

(743) Gaten thinks that luck plays a big part in acting. Where it not for the Duffers creating Stranger Things and enjoying his auditions he might never have got a major break in television and my even have drifted out of acting.

(744) In an episode of The Simpsons, Homer watched a Stranger Things parody called Odder Stuff.

(745) The boys refer to proton packs on their Ghostbusters costumes in Stranger Things 2. This is a mistake because that term was only used in the 1989 sequel. The correct term in 1984 would have been positron colliders.

(746) Stranger Things was nominated for a 2017 BAFTA in the best international show category.

(747) The Stranger Things title graphic is instantly nostalgic because large typefaces were very popular in the 1980s.

(748) There have been a number of Stranger Things jigsaw puzzles.

(749) Limahl said the American interest in the NeverEnding Story song after Stranger Things 3 was satisfying because the United States was one of the few places where the song hadn't been a hit in 1984.

(750) Shawn Levy said that he would be disappointed if

anyone DIDN'T binge watch Stranger Things. That's exactly what it was designed for.

(751) Finn Wolfhard said the Dustin and Suzie NeverEnding story duet in Stranger Things 3 is his favourite scene so far in the show. Finn also loved the fact that the other characters thought Dustin's girlfriend was fictitious but she turned out to be real.

(752) There is a now a Stranger Things Trivial Pursuit with questions all about the 1980s.

(753) A Stranger Things Edition Polaroid Camera was released in 2019. It was priced at $99.

(754) Explaining his decision to take a summer job (despite being a famous actor), Gaten said - "Over the summer during the pandemic, there were a couple of restaurants near where I live in New Jersey that were open because they all had outdoor seating. Both of my siblings got a job at this place, a couple of my friends, some of my cousins did too, so everybody I've ever known and met and talked to. I was sitting on the couch one day and my brother was like 'Going to work. See you at like 11 p.m.' and I was like 'OK.' And he leaves and I'm playing Mario Kart and I'm still playing Mario Kart, and then after a while I'm still playing Mario Kart. So I got really good at it to the point at which I knew it was sad. I'm like 'Wow I'm good. I need to stop.' So I'm like if they're all leaving, they're the only people I know, I might just follow and go with them, and so I did."

(755) Gaten said that Ron Weasley is his favourite character in Harry Potter.

(756) Gaten said of Dustin Henderson - "I like how he's

loyal to his friends and he's always there to keep trying to get people to get along, even if it doesn't work out all that well. He's always trying his best to keep everyone in line."

(757) Gaten said that Millie Bobby Brown was very shy when he first met her at the Stranger Things auditions. He says she is the complete opposite of shy now!

(758) Gaten and the other Stranger Things teenagers are often seen at Six flags amusement park in Georgia when Stranger things is in production. This theme park is only a twenty minute drive from Atlanta.

(759) Six flags amusement park has a spooky Stranger Things maze. Gaten has sampled this attraction himself.

(760) Gaten says him and the other Stranger Things kids would sometimes have food fights away from the camera in the early seasons. There were plenty of hijinks on the set.

(761) Gaten said the cast and crew felt a lot of pressure making Stranger Things 2 because the expectations were very high after all the acclaim for season one.

(762) Gaten said that secrecy measures to preserve spoilers on Stranger Things 2 became a bit paranoid in the end and everyone became worried there was a 'mole' in the crew leaking information!

(763) Gaten said the first musical he ever watched was a production of Annie that his sister was in.

(764) Gaten said that because of his experience from Broadway he doesn't suffer from stage fright when he performs with his band Work in Progress. He has plenty

of previous experience when it comes to a live audience.

(765) Gaten is a fan of Mac DeMarco.

(766) Gaten says one of the things he likes most about the Six Flags theme parks is that the food is pretty good.

(767) Gaten was specially trained in vocal methods to look after his voice while on Broadway. He still adheres to these methods.

(768) Gaten is a fan of Jimmy Hendrix.

(769) Gaten says that on Stranger Things the cast never get to see any scripts until they arrive in Atlanta to commence shooting.

(770) Gaten teamed up with Verizon to help raise funds for first responders through the Gary Sinise Foundation.

(771) Gaten is a fan of fruit juice.

(772) Gaten became an "honorary toy" during his visit to Toy Story Land at Disney's Hollywood Studios in 2019.

(773) Gaten said he was once mobbed by a crowd of fans while at Universal Orlando.

(774) In Katy Perry's Swish Swish music video, Gaten played Perry's teammate on the comical Tigers basketball team.

(775) Gaten said the scene where Dustin and Steve bond while in the woods leaving a trail of meat for Dart in Stranger Things 2 is one of his favourite scenes in any season of the show.

(776) Gaten wore an eggplant-colour suit and black bowtie for junior prom.

(777) Gaten is partial to an ice cream sundae.

(778) Gaten said that, in the wake of season one of Stranger Things dropping on Netflix, it was definitely a strange experience when people began asking for his autograph for the first time. It was very strange to wake up one day and suddenly be famous.

(779) Gaten says he sometimes forgets that he is famous!

(780) Gaten says he can do a few Michael Jackson dance moves.

(781) When Gaten was first cast in Stranger Things he and the kids went to the cinema together as a bonding exercise.

(782) Gaten said that on the first of shooting on Stranger Things the boys all got the giggles because Finn Wolfhard sneezed during a take.

(783) Gaten is hopeful that his days of numerous surgeries for cleidocranial dysplasia might be over. He thinks the worst is behind him now.

(784) Gaten says that while cleidocranial dysplasia made it more difficult for him to get parts at first it worked to his advantage in the end and helped him to land a part in Stranger Things.

(785) Gaten says he prefers to think of those with cleidocranial dysplasia as special and distinctive rather

than people suffering from an affliction or medical problem.

(786) Gaten said that being away from school and having a private tutor during the production of Stranger Things took some getting used to but it all worked out fine in the end.

(787) Gaten says he is a bit of a hoarder. He still has some old games and toys from his childhood.

(788) Gaten says he keeps up to date with the careers of the other kids in Stranger Things and is proud of their accomplishments.

(789) Gaten tends to wear his hair shorter in real life than Dustin Henderson does in Stranger Things.

(790) As a science fiction and horror buff, Stranger Things was obviously right up Gaten's alley.

(791) Gaten said he has learned a lot about directing and film and television production while working on Stranger Things.

(792) Gaten has done an awful lot of radio interviews in his duties promoting Stranger Things.

(793) Gaten said he is very happy in New Jersey with his friends and family. He hasn't felt the need to move for the sake of his career. Being so close to New York makes the need to move less important.

(794) Gaten is a big fan of the city of Dallas.

(795) Gaten tends to be known as a comedic actor but he

thinks he could do a purely dramatic straight performance if a part required it.

(796) Gaten said he got into theatre because he wanted to be like his sister.

(797) The melty, sticky, and icky nature of the monster special effects in Stranger Things 3 take some inspiration from the (cheesy but fun and gruesome) 1988 remake of The Blob. The remake of The Blob has a number of similarities with Stranger Things 3. It has a small town atmosphere, a sheriff, and some horror scenes in a hospital. The home of the heroine Shawnee Smith in The Blob looks a lot like the Wheeler house inside and the hero Kevin Dillon has an outrageous mullet like Billy Hargrove. The Blob remake also naturally has mysterious government scientists in hazmat suits. It even has kids being smuggled into a cinema to watch a horror film and then the movie cutting out because of an inexplicable event. The military scientists in The Blob want to get hold of the organism to use as a biological weapon. This is sort of what the Soviets are trying to do in Stranger Things 3. Given all the similarities, you would be amazed if the Duffers had never watched The Blob remake.

(798) The Duffers wanted us to see more of the home life of Lucas and Dustin in Stranger Things 2. We never saw them at home in the first season.

(799) The overnight fame Stranger Things bestowed on most of the cast was something that some embraced more than others. Millie Bobby Brown seemed to be having the time of her life whereas the very private Natalia Dyer took to wearing a hat in public so she wouldn't be recognised. Gaten was somewhere in the middle when it came to dealing with fame.

(800) In reality, Maxine Mayfield would not have had enough characters available to enter 'MADMAX' into Dig Dug's high score gallery in Stranger Things 2. This is what you might call a very minor mistake (for artistic licence). You'd have to be an expert on eighties video game arcades to notice.

(801) You can see yellow road lines in Stranger Things but road lines in Indiana were white at the time the show takes place.

(802) Many stores you see at the Starcourt Mall in Stranger Things 3 like Sam Goody, Wicks N' Sticks, Waldenbooks, and Hot Sam Pretzels, are now defunct and no longer exist.

(803) When they were still pitching Stranger Things, the Duffers cut together a concept trailer composed of classic eighties film clips backed with a John Carpenter score. Although there were no scripts when the actors were cast, the actors were all shown the test trailer the Duffers had designed using iconic moments from 1980s fantasy movies. The actors therefore understood what the Duffers were trying to do and were excited about the potential of the concept. Gaten said he genuinely had no idea if Stranger Things would be successful but he did think that it could be cool and exciting.

(804) The Upside Down, the mysterious, dangerous, and desolate area opened by the dimensional rift in Stranger Things, was known as the Nether in the scripts when season one was in production. This was later changed because the Duffers got tired of hearing jokes about 'nether regions'. They thought the Upside Down was a much better name so the Nether officially became the

Upside Down. The Upside Down was not supposed to feature much in the original plans for Stranger Things. It was supposed to be a place that was largely unseen and would have to be imagined by the audience. A place of Lovecraft inspired horror that would be too terrifying to endure or show.

(805) The comic con trailer for Stranger Things 2 in 2017 was one of the greatest TV or film trailers in recent memory. Shawn Levy spent two months wrangling with the lawyers of the Michael Jackson estate to gain permission to use the song Thriller in the trailer. It was not so much Michael Jackson that Levy wanted but the atmospheric intro and the opening narration by the legendary horror icon Vincent Price. This proved the perfect audio backdrop for the amazing Halloween themed trailer and anticipation for Stranger Things 2, already considerable, was now stratospheric. The Stranger Things 2 'Thriller' trailer soon became legendary and amassed millions of views. It began with Dragon's Lair animation and showed Will Byers finding himself in a terrifying Upside Down arcade before catching a glimpse of the Flayer in the red electrical sky.

(806) Mr Clarke uses an analogy in Stranger Things to explain superstring theory and the multiverse to Dustin and the boys when they ask him questions about other dimensions at the funeral of Will Byers. He tells them to imagine an acrobat on a rope. The acrobat can only go back and forwards. Then imagine a flea on the rope. The flea can go anywhere. It can even move around and come back to where it started. The flea had access to a dimension that the acrobat didn't.

(807) Cleidocranial dysplasia doesn't affect cognition and physical aptitude.

(808) Gaten played played Benji on the stage in Priscilla, Queen of the Desert. This show was based on the 1994 film.

(809) Gaten takes a size six shoe.

(810) Gaten helped to support a nonprofit restaurant called Soul Kitchen. The donated proceeds go toward helping individuals struggling with food insecurity.

(811) Gaten says the Stranger Things kids played a lot of Monopoly between filming on the first two seasons.

(812) Gaten said he asked for Dustin to have a dog in Stranger Things 2 but the Duffers gave Dustin an Upside Down creature as a pet instead!

(813) Gaten's role in The Blacklist was as a kid who has been brainwashed by a cult group. It was quite a dark role.

(814) Netflix dubbed Stranger Things into nine languages and subtitled it in twenty-two. This made the show more accessible in international markets.

(815) The Body of Stranger Things takes its title from the Stephen King novella which was adapted into the classic Rob Reiner film Stand By Me.

(816) The restaurant chain Lucky Chip created some Stranger Things themed treats when season one was a big hit. These included the Ryder Vegetarian Burger and Eleven's Onion Rings.

(817) In an IGN poll, the first season of Stranger Things

was voted the best season. It took 53% of the votes.

(818) The product visibility in season three of Stranger Things was valued at $15 million. There is no actual product placement though and no company paid any money to be in the show.

(819) Chester Rushing, who played Tommy in the first two seasons, said there was a palpable electricity at the first ever Stranger Things cast reading.

(820) Joe Keery describes the Steve and Dustin duo in Stranger Things as like The Odd Couple!

(821) The school dance at the end of the John Hughes film Sixteen Candles was one of the main inspirations for the Snow Ball at the end of Stranger Things 2.

(822) Stranger Things has some vague spiritual connections to the 1984 film The Last Starfighter. In both Stranger Things and The Last Starfighter, an aptitude and knowledge of games becomes a tool through which to arm one's self for a real life adventure and quest.

(823) The Snow Ball dance at the end of Stranger Things 2 clearly takes some inspiration from the Enchantment Under the Sea dance in Back to the Future.

(824) One might argue that Gaten has already displayed his dramatic acting chops with his role in The Blacklist. He is a much more versatile actor than one might think.

(825) Gaten said he would like to do some musical theatre workshops to keep his hand lest he should return to the stage.

(826) Where Gaten grew up in Jersey was about two hours away from New York and Broadway.

(827) Because of Stranger Things the fame of Gaten has spread to many countries around the world.

(828) Gaten is a fan of puzzles.

(829) There is obviously a lot of Stranger Things merch (action figures, hoodies, etc, etc) now available. It is not known if Gaten and the cast on a certain percentage of the profits of this merch but one would imagine they are as in many cases a likeness of them is used.

(830) Gaten formed something of a double act with Caleb McLaughlin in the early promotional tours for Stranger Things. They did a lot of interviews together.

(831) Though he is now nineteen Gaten hasn't ruled out taking more educational classes in the future.

(832) Gaten, immersed in eighties movies and horror and science fiction as he is, thinks he is pretty good at picking up all the Easter eggs and pop culture references in Stranger Things.

(833) Gaten is a fan of comic books.

(834) Stranger Things 3 can be commended for the way that it writes in the fact that the younger cast members are now teenagers rather than little kids. Mike and Lucas are more interested in girls than games and while Dustin retains his childlike enthusiasm for the world he's also been away at camp and got a girlfriend of his own.

(835) For a special night, Gaten took over Netflix's

Instagram account for the 2016 Emmy's.

(836) Gaten, as we have seen, has used his fame as a platform to support many worthwhile causes. He thinks this is one of the positive aspects of being famous and one that makes it all worthwhile in the end.

(837) Eonline.com called Gaten one of the nicest celebrities in the business. One of the main things they cited was his willingness to have photographs taken with fns.

(838) Stranger Things casting director Carmen Cuba says that casting kids for a film or television show can be a delicate and tough task at times. "I've had young actors leave auditions and later be told that they were very upset. Being a mom I am extra sensitive to kids--it's a very hard thing to do, to go into a room and really be tested on hard material--but other people in the room aren't always in tune with the fact that these kids are really putting it on the line for them and that it's hard emotionally. But it's a business, unfortunately, and kid actors are a tricky thing on lots of levels."

(839) Netflix does not comment on the salaries of the actors in Stranger Things but Deadline reported, as we noted earlier, that the 'kids' in the show had negotiated substantial pay rises for season three. It was speculated though by the site that Millie Bobby Brown, the biggest star out of the younger cast members, would receive the largest pay increase.

(840) Gaten said he enjoys vegetables - which is obviously good given their health benefits!

(841) According to the votes on Ranker, the three best

episodes of Stranger Things are The Battle of Starcourt, The Upside Down, and The Gate.

(842) Vinnie's Pizzeria in Brooklyn, New York, celebrated the success of the first season of the show in 2016 by creating some Stranger Things themed pizzas and dishes.

(843) Gaten's favourite colour is blue.

(844) Gaten thinks he can do a good impression of Millie Bobby Brown's English accent!

(845) Gaten is a fan of the TV show American Horror Story.

(846) Hasbro has released a Stranger Things Dungeons & Dragons Starter Set. In the game you can embark on a Dungeons & Dragons adventure and hunt for the Thessalhydra in a campaign.

(847) It says something for the great chemistry between Joe Keery and Gaten that we hardly notice the fact that Dustin is separated from the other kids for most of Stranger Things 3.

(848) Gaten says that despite his cleidocranial dysplasia he is still able to do most of the things that normal kids and teenagers do.

(849) Gaten is a fan of the TV show Arrow.

(850) Some fans think that Stranger Things 2 missed a trick by not having Polybius in the Palace Arcade. Polybius is a fictitious arcade game and the subject of an urban myth. The urban legend describes the game as part of a government-run psychology experiment based in

Portland, Oregon, during 1981. Gameplay supposedly produced intense psychoactive and addictive effects in the player.

(851) Gaten's favourite season is the summer. He also likes the fall.

(852) Gaten lives about twenty minutes away from the beach.

(853) Erica in Stranger Things 3 is a My Little Pony fan - which, as Dustin amusingly points out, makes her something of a nerd!

(854) Gaten enjoys surfing at the beach when there are good waves and the weather is warm. He also likes boogie boarding.

(855) Gaten said he is a big fan of cheese.

(856) Gaten likes playing spikeball with his friends. Spikeball is a team sport played by two teams of two players. Opposing teams line up across from each other with the Spikeball net in the center. The ball is put in play with a serve—a hit by the server from behind the service boundary into the net to an opposing player. Once the ball is served players can move anywhere they want. The object of the game is to hit the ball into the net so that the opposing team cannot return it.

(857) Catherine Curtin, who plays Dustin's mother in Stranger Things, says she loves the dynamic the two characters have. "And I kind of love how with Dustin's mom, in a way, Dustin is taking charge. I sort of love that power dynamic, where the mother is so in love with the son that the stars and the moon align with his actions."

(858) The music website (and former magazine) NME
(New Musical Express) ranked Finn Wolfhard's Calpurnia
as the best of the various bands that Stranger Things cast
members have been part of.

(859) Gaten likes noodles.

(860) When he was a kid on Broadway, Gaten was limited
in how many shows he could do because of child labour
laws.

(861) Gaten said that him and the cast try to have fun
making Stranger Things because it makes the work
environment better and gives the show a nice energy that
hopefully translates to the audience.

(862) Gaten likes Perogies. Pierogi are filled dumplings
made by wrapping unleavened dough around a savoury or
sweet filling and cooking in boiling water.

(863) The release of Stranger Things 3 in 2019 saw the
return of New Coke in a cross-promotion between Netflix
and Coca-Cola. Those who sampled the drink seemed to
be rather lukewarm in their reviews. The general
consensus is that New Coke is sweeter and more 'generic'
tasting than 'Classic' Coca-Cola.

(864) Gaten is a fan of the film Jurassic Park.

(865) Gaten said it was a great relief to finally finish
shooting Stranger Things 4 because the production had
been so stop-start and lengthy due to the pandemic.

(866) Gaten says that when he finishes shooting a season
on Stranger Things the first thing he does is get his hair

cut because he finds Dustin's long hair to be a pain in real life.

(867) Gaten feels that giving Dustin a disability (cleidocranial dysplasia) made him more relatable as a character.

(868) Gaten thinks that Dustin has matured over the course of Stranger Things.

(869) Gaten loves the musical Sweeney Todd.

(870) 2019 saw the release of Stranger Things: The Upside Down Lego set. This 2,300-piece Lego set recreates both the regular and Upside Down versions of Hawkins.

(871) Gaten is a big fan of the musical Spring Awakening.

(872) That's the Farrah Fawcett hairspray from Stranger Things 2 that Dustin uses on Lucas in Stranger Things 3 after Eleven spooks him by making his toys come to life as a prank.

(873) Gaten said shooting the scenes at the end of Stranger Things 2 where Steve and the kids escape from the flame festooned tunnels was super tiring and tough because it was near the end of a long shoot and 4am in the morning when they finished!

(874) Gaten said the Dungeons & Dragons game which begins (after the prologue in the lab) season one Stranger Things was his favourite scene to shoot in the show so far.

(875) Gaten is a fan of the television show The Flash.

(876) Fans have suggested that Gaten would make a good Shaggy in Scooby Doo.

(877) Gaten's favourite type of omelette is a vegetable omelette with cheddar cheese.

(878) Michael Stein and Kyle Dixon of the electronic synth group Survive (S U R V I V E) were chosen to compose the score for Stranger Things. The Duffers were impressed by their work on the offbeat 2014 thriller film The Guest. As a test, they had taken out the John Carpenter music on their Montauk pitch trailer and replaced it with music by Survive. It was a perfect match. Stein and Dixon were brought in before a single frame of Stranger Things had been shot. They even supplied some music that the Duffers and Carmen Cuba could put over the actor audition scenes.

(879) The green gloop in vials that Dustin and the 'Scoop Troop' find in the underground base in Stranger Things 3 could be a reference to John Carpenter's 1987 film Prince of Darkness. In the film, scientists encounter the essence of the devil (in the form of a green liquid) in an old church.

(880) Dustin's mother has a yellow Volvo 244 sedan in Stranger Things 3.

(881) Gaten said his favourite character in Stranger Things is Murray Bauman and he loves working with Bret Gelman (who obviously plays Murray in the show).

(882) Gaten feels that Stranger Things has an appealing element in that the 'geeks' are the heroes and bullies are the villains.

(883) Gaten's girlfriend Lizzy Yu has performed in various theatre dramas like The Outsiders and Cinderella.

(884) According to the United States National Library of Medicine, one in a million individuals worldwide have cleidocranial dysplasia.

(885) Suzie is reading Ursula K. Le Guin's novel A Wizard Of Earthsea when Dustin finally manages to make contact with her in Stranger Things 3.

(886) Sean Astin said that, as a former child actor himself, he could relate to Gaten and the kids in Stranger Things and ended up sharing some of his own experiences to them on the set of Stranger Things 2

(887) The candy store It'Sugar also offered some Stranger Things themed treats by creating Gummy Eggos and Missing Barb's Malted Milk Balls.

(888) The green gloop in the vials that the Scoop Troop find in the Soviet base in Stranger Things 3 turns out to be acidic. This is a reference to the Alien series.

(889) Gaten says he does his best to drink water rather than soda with his meals.

(890) Dustin's mother has a bobble head version of Mews the cat on the dashboard of her car in Stranger Things 3.

(891) It would have cost around $4,000 to buy a Dragon's Lair arcade machine in 1984.

(892) A possible source of inspiration for the Demogorgon in Stranger Things is Parasyte - a science fiction horror manga series written and illustrated by

Hitoshi Iwaaki

(893) The building used for the Starcourt Mall in Stranger Things 3 is Gwinnett Place Mall - located in the Pleasant Hill Road corridor of Duluth, Georgia.

(894) 2019 saw the release of Stranger Things 3: The Game. This video game was released on Nintendo Switch, Xbox One, PlayStation 4, Mac, PC, iOS and Android. The 16 bit retro game got quite middling reviews when it came out. In the game you explore Hawkins and solve puzzles. There are twelve characters from the show to play in the game.

(895) According to Parrot Analytics, over the four-day period of its initial release, Stranger Things 3 registered 3.2 times the 'demand expressions' of Game of Thrones.

(896) Kyle Hill of Nerdist has said that it would not be impossible for something like the Upside Down in Stranger Things to really exist.

(897) There are video game fans who think Stranger Things might have been partly inspired by Half-Life. Half-Life is a classic 1998 first-person shooter video game developed by Valve and published by Sierra Studios for Microsoft Windows in 1998.

(898) Gaten is a fan of tiramisu. Tiramisu is a coffee-flavoured Italian dessert. It is made of ladyfingers dipped in coffee, layered with a whipped mixture of eggs, sugar, and mascarpone cheese, flavoured with cocoa.

(899) Gaten has a few Spider-Man t-shirts that he likes to wear.

(900) The Stranger Things kids sing a song called the
Chicken noodle song backstage while shooting Stranger
Things. Caleb made up the song to annoy Gaten and Sadie
Sink!

(901) Project MKUltra plays an important in season of
Stranger Things. Project MKUltra was a top secret CIA
funded experiment into mind control that made use of
the mind-altering drug LSD. MKUltra was a response to
American fears that the Soviets were more advanced in
brainwashing and mind control techniques. The MKUltra
experiments included remote viewing and extrasensory
perception. While these things were never proven to be
real, the actual experiments did actually happen. Project
MKUltra ended in 1973 and only became public
knowledge after the experiment was terminated.

(902) According to an online calculator, Gaten gets on
average about 953,362 likes per Instagram post.

(903) The Duffers had very briefly considered pitching
Montauk as a proposed film when they first had the idea
but they always felt it would be much better as a
miniseries or TV show. It is possible (though no sure
thing) that they could have secured some funding to make
Montauk as a movie but Stranger Things (as it would
become) was clearly much better suited to be a television
show. Think of all the great moments in Stranger Things
we would have missed out on if the eight hours of story
had been condensed down into a two hour or 100 minute
movie script!

(904) Gaten is a fan of Linguine.

(905) The aim of the Duffers was to make Stranger
Things akin to a PG-13 film that could be enjoyed by all

ages but might be too scary for younger children. However, the Duffers did not feel constricted or bound by this general ambition and were prepared to 'push' the audience with some grisly horror if the mood took them. T

(906) Gaten teamed up with Michelle Obama in her new Netflix kids show Waffles and Mochi in 2017. Waffles and Mochi is a cartoon about food around the world.

(907) Brookhaven National Laboratory (in Upton, NY) is another facility that could have provided some inspiration for Stranger Things. This lab is owned by the U.S. Department of Energy and most definitely not open to the public. It engages in all manner of remarkable scientific experiments and has a Relativistic Heavy Ion Collider which is used to learn more about dark matter and the nature of the universe.

(908) Gaten is a big fan of mushrooms.

(909) Dungeons & Dragons was subject to legal action from the Tolkien estate for its similarities to Lord of the Rings and The Hobbit.

(910) Gaten is a fan of The Beatles.

(911) Gaten feels that the early death of Barb Holland in Stranger Things, though sad, was necessary in a narrative sense because it made the audience feel that none of the characters were safe and therefore (hopefully) gave the show more tension as a viewing experience.

(912) Gaten said he doesn't like being alone.

(913) The 1985 Joe Dante film Explorers is another

children's adventure movie that Stranger Things shares
DNA with in a way that is not immediately obvious.
Explorers is about three children (who include a young
Ethan Hawke and River Phoenix in their film debuts) who
encounter aliens when they travel into outer space by
means of a space craft that they somehow fashion
themselves. Spielberg. The boys in Explorers love science
and it is their love of science and open-mindedness (a
very childlike quality that adults tend to lose) that makes
the adventure come to them. These are elements we see
very much in evidence with the boys in Stranger Things.

(914) One of Gaten's dogs is called Rocky.

(915) Gaten says he likes waffles. This is a contrast to
Millie Bobby Brown - who can take or leave them despite
playing the waffle loving Eleven in Stranger Things.

(916) Gaten said the kids in Stranger Things like to
decorate their trailers when a season is in production.

(917) Arcade historians thought that the most unrealistic
thing about the Palace Arcade in Stranger Things 2 was
how clean and bright it looked. A busy eighties arcade,
with a high turnover of children and teenagers, would
almost certainly have been more grubby and arcades
didn't tend to waste too much money on décor or lighting.
You could explain away the Palace Arcade appearing so
pristine and bright by the fact that it seems to be a
relatively new business in Hawkins.

(918) Gaten said he especially liked making Stranger
Things 4 because he was legally no longer a minor and so
there were no restrictions on what hours or times he
could work.

(919) The villain of Stranger Things 2 is the Mind Flayer -
an unspecified big boss of the Upside Down. The
manifestation of the creature is visually inspired by
electric storms and volcanoes. The Duffers said that
Voldemort in Harry Potter and the stories of Clive Barker
were an influence on the Mind Flayer. The Flayer is a
horror that can't be readily explained.

(920) Gaten said he had long days working on Stranger
Things 4. Some days he would arrive at 8am and wouldn't
get to go home until 8pm.

(921) The Mind Flayer is also clearly inspired by
Lovecraft's cosmic entity Cthulhu.

(922) Gaten said the kids (now teenagers of course) in
Stranger Things sometimes buy one another gifts.

(923) Video game fans have remarked on a similarity
between the Flayer in Stranger Things and Amygdala
from the game Bloodborne.

(924) Season two costume designer Kim Wilcox
researched Tiger Beat and Cosmopolitan magazines, as
well as old Sears and J.C. Penney's catalogues for
Stranger Things 2.

(925) The Halloween scenes in Stranger Things 2 of the
boys out in their Ghostbusters costumes seem to owe
something to Trick 'r Treat. Trick 'r Treat is a very
underrated 2007 horror anthology film by Michael
Dougherty that presents five interlocking stories set at
Halloween in the same small town.

(926) The Farrah Fawcett spray that Steve and Dustin use
in Stranger Things 2 was a real product by Faberge Inc.

Steve would be dismayed to learn though that it was discontinued in 1984.

(927) Characters use polaroid cameras in Stranger Things 2. These cameras - while basic by today's standards - were quite a novelty in the eighties because you didn't have to take your photographs away to be developed.

(928) You don't really see much evidence of the boys in Stranger Things using a computer or playing video games at home. You would expect a science nerd like Dustin to have a home computer and the Wheeler family certainly seem wealthy enough to have a high end (for the time) computer. We did see in season one that Will Byers seemed quite excited at the thought that one of his Christmas presents might be an Atari. Computer and gaming historians think it most likely that, in the early eighties, boys like this would have owned a Commodore 64.

(929) The Police song Every Breath You Take you hear right at the end of Stranger Things 2 is not a love song but a song about stalking. The message of this song at the end is that - despite the happy ending at the Snowball - the Mind Flayer is still there and still stalking the plucky residents of Hawkins. Gaten said he finds this song very creepy.

(930) Stranger Things has been happily free of scandal and behind the scenes problems in the course of its history and production. You really don't have to go too far at all to encounter television shows (Desperate Housewives, Sex and the City, even, believe it or not, The Golden Girls) which had to deal with some feuding actors who didn't get on at all. Actors have been fired from TV shows for feuds with producers or scandals in their past.

You can list a number of high profile TV shows that had to axe or recast a character because of some offscreen scandal or dispute. Stranger Things has, happily, not encountered any of these problems. The cast seem to be one big happy family and there have been no reports of discord or feuds among the cast.

(931) Joe Keery, Maya Hawke, Gaten, and Priah Ferguson spent much of the production of Stranger Things 3 away from the main cast shooting their scenes of the Scoop Troop's adventures in the Russian base. The four of them formed a close bond during the shoot. Joe Keery said they all got on well and had a lot of fun.

(932) The casting of Winona Ryder in Stranger Things happily mitigated any desire Netflix might have had to pursue better known actors for the other parts. This allowed the Duffers and their casting director to cast who they wanted - even if those people were complete unknowns who hadn't done anything else.

(933) The Mall Rats episode of Stranger Things mentions telephone numbers in the 765 area code. In 1985 though it would have been area code 317 in Indiana.

(934) The blue/white flashlight beams in Stranger Things season one are not correct for the era. Flashlights from this era had an orange/yellow glow.

(935) In Stranger Things 2, we see that Dustin has a Wheel of Fortune board game in his house.

(936) Gaten says he dislikes the 'f-word' - the f-word in this case being fame.

(937) Gaten is a fan of lasagna.

(938) Dustin's pet DemoDog Dart in Stranger Things 2 trades on the Joe Dante film Gremlins but also has something of Ridley Scott's Alien in the manner that the creature sheds its skin and grows very rapidly.

(939) Stephen King's Firestarter is one of the most obvious influences on Stranger Things. The plot revolves around a young girl who has pyrokinetic abilities because her parents were subject to an MKUltra type experiment when they were teenagers.

(940) David Harbour says of life on the Stranger Things set with the kids that - "Sometimes when they get a little out of hand, I also am the guy who's able to be on set saying, "All right, come on kids, let's get down to work." So in some ways I'm a cool uncle, and in some ways I'm like a nasty physics teacher."

(941) Stranger Things merchandise includes a Steve Harrington Babysitter's Club bag and an Eggo card game.

(942) Dustin brings some Bazooka bubble gum as part of his food package when the boys decide to search for Will again in season one of Stranger Things. This brand of bubble gum was first marketed in 1947.

(943) Gaten says the most of the music he listens to at home is from musical theatre.

(944) When Steve and Dustin and the kids take refuge in the bus in the junkyard during Stranger Things 2 this might be another reference to the Mad Max film series - where vehicles are fortified to survive in a post apocalyptic future. MADMAX is the username of Max Mayfield in the arcade.

(945) Gaten said he is proud of his natural curls.

(946) The families of the cast members are not allowed to read the Stranger Things scripts for fear of spoilers or hackers.

(947) For the season two marketing, Netflix released a Stranger Things YouTube playlist called Hawkins Monitored where you could spy on various characters through surveillance footage.

(948) Gaten said - "Everybody is different in their own unique way and everybody is hiding something deep down and if they could open up they would feel more confident in who they actually are."

(949) The research of Netflix on viewing habits of Stranger Things found that the second episode was the one that 'hooked' viewers. Those who made it to the second episode overwhelmingly went on to watch the rest of the season.

(950) Stranger Things is not really constructed as a conventional season of long form television. A season of Stranger Things is constructed as a (very long) movie.

(951) Cleidocranial dysplasia makes Dustin a target for school bullies in Stranger Things but he's a cheerful and dogged sort of chap who usually manages to overcome the obstacles that life hurls at him. One could say the same of Gaten.

(952) In 2021, Gaten appeared on The Burger Show and helped to create a special Stranger Things burger.

(953) Gaten has a Brontosaure Hoodie as Dustin season two of Stranger things.

(954) Gaten's Pokémon team is team valor - the red team.

(955) Gaten said he tried to buy a Dungeons & Dragons set when he was cast in Stranger Things but he couldn't find one in the shops anywhere and had to resort to ebay.

(956) Gaten said that playing Dustin in Stranger Things is no great stretch because he feels as if he is essentially just playing himself in the show most of the time.

(957) Gaten said that his siblings get on very well with his girlfriend Lizzie Yu.

(958) Gaten spent New Year's Eve 2017 in Times Square.

(959) Gaten has attended a comic con in Spain.

(960) Gaten met John Boyega at the Rise of Skywalker premiere.

(961) Gaten is a fan of the Will Ferrell film Elf.

(962) Gaten has taken part in campaigns which encourage young people to vote in elections.

(963) Gaten has lent his support to the Black Lives Matter movement.

(964) Gaten has appeared on the cover of 1883 Magazine.

(965) Gaten says that his grandpa makes the best pizza.

(966) Gaten says that people always pester him for

Stranger Things spoilers but he is of course sworn to secrecy.

(967) Gaten said he enjoys all the elaborate Stranger Things fan theories and always keeps up to date with them.

(968) Gaten is a big fan of the Star Wars film Rogue One.

(969) Gaten thinks that because of social media and the internet people don't talk to each other face to face as much as they used to in eras less festooned with technology. He thinks this is a shame.

(970) Shooting Stranger Things 4 was quite complex according to Gaten because of the pandemic protocols. The cast had to wear masks on the set and be separated during lunch.

(971) Gaten said it was great to see everyone again at the table read for Stranger Things 4 because they all felt as if they had been apart for far too long.

(972) In 2019, a Stranger Things Pop-Up Experience opened at Universal's Cabana Bay Beach Resort.

(973) Gaten wore a yellow Dolce & Gabbana jacket at the 2018 Emmys.

(974) Gaten is a fan of Shore Good Donuts in Long Beach.

(975) Gaten took his mother to the Golden Globe Awards.

(976) Gaten is a fan of swimming pools. He says he always takes his swimming costume with him everywhere.

(977) Gaten is a fan of French food.

(978) Gaten said that one of the biggest changes Stranger Things made to his life is that it gave him the chance to travel to many different places he might not have seen otherwise.

(979) Gaten said he would love to be a wizard in real life.

(980) In 2019, Men's Health ranked Dustin Henderson as the second best character in Stranger Things. Steve Harrington topped the poll.

(981) A 2020 poll in LadBible ranked Stranger Things as the best Netflix show. It took 53% of the vote.

(982) A Screenrant poll in 2020 ranked Dustin Henderson as the fifth most likeable character in Stranger Things.

(983) Asked which superpower he would like to have, Gaten said that he would like the ability to fly.

(984) You can buy a LEGO mini Dustin Henderson figure.

(985) Gaten has some orange laced footwear in Stranger Things 3.

(986) Dustin's love of Three Musketeers candy is a twist on kids usually being disappointed at Halloween if they get too many of them. Some feel that a Three Musketeers is just a Snickers with all the good stuff taken out.

(987) As a period piece, Stranger Things posed a great

challenge to the props and fashion department. The prop master was Lynda Reiss. The approach was to recreate the era as if from memory. They didn't want Stranger Things to feel like a nostalgia piece but rather something that felt real. They wanted Stranger Things to feel like someone in the present day watching a movie made in 1983. If something was not 100% authentic to the era though it didn't matter as long as it felt right. The occasional anachronism would be no big deal and was probably unavoidable.

(988) The building used to depict the Hawkins Department of Energy in Stranger Things is an abandoned mental institution in Atlanta.

(989) Dustin's pet Dart in Stranger Things 2 was voiced by sound designer Craig Henighan.

(990) Hasbro released a Stranger Things Ouija board game based on the Christmas light scenes in season one.

(991) When we see the Wheeler family eating with Dustin as a guest in season one of Stranger Things, they are having meatloaf, mashed potato and green beans.

(992) When it comes to Stranger Things cast members, Gaten isn't alone in wanting to be in Star Wars. Millie Bobby Brown says her dream role is to play young Princess Leia in a Star Wars film.

(993) The Lovecraft story which has the most similarities with Stranger Things is From Beyond. The book was published in 1920 and is about dark secret dimensions unknown to man.

(994) Stranger Things fan theories really started to go

haywire around the time of season two. The theories are always fun to read even if most of them have no validity when it comes to what the Duffers actually intended or might be planning. The most far out theories included the suggestion that the Demogorgon was Will Byers from the future. If this sounds unlikely then even more unlikely was the theory that the Mind Flayer was an evil Upside Down version of Barb. The theory that the Upside Down is a version of Hawkins ruined by nuclear war is a popular (and slightly more plausible) theory. In this theory, the Demogorgons would be humans who had evolved and mutated in the fallout. The most obvious problem with this theory is that it doesn't explain what the Mind Flayer might be or where that came from.

(995) In 2021, Gaten celebrated his third year anniversary with girlfriend Lizzie Yu.

(996) Gaten calls his girlfriend Lizzie Yu his 'sunshine'.

(997) When he landed a role on Broadway, Gaten's supportive mother personally drove him to New York each day for his shows and rehearsals.

(998) Gaten has supported the campaign to limit plastic pollution.

(999) Gaten says that unlike Dustin Henderson he doesn't really wear hats or caps in real life.

(1000) Gaten says that being cast in Stranger Things definitely changed his life in a remarkable way.

Other Books by Mera Wolfe

1000 Millie Bobby Brown Facts

1000 Harry Potter Facts

1000 Billie Eilish Facts

1000 Ariana Grande Facts

1000 Friends Facts

1000 Finn Wolfhard Facts